The Incarnation
in a Divided World

Donald DeMarco

Christendom College Press
Front Royal, Virginia

Contents

Foreword

In writing this book, Donald DeMarco has accomplished something that is all too rare these days: he has produced an analysis of the fundamental divisions in our world that does not in itself contribute to the deepening of those divisions. It is one measure of how far our civilization has strayed from the true sources of order that even the sincere aspirations of millions of men and women to see these divisions healed are compromised by our modern confusions of mind and spirit. Take, for example, the peace movement. The emotional fervor of those who march or sing for peace is often admirable and even moving. But the notion that peace could be achieved only by dismantling the "military-industrial complex" overlooks the reality of evil and the intractability of human conflicts.

It is the tendency to overlook, or turn away from, one aspect of reality in order to emphasize another that the Church has called "heresy." Heresy is a form of one-sidedness, a hope that in the face of the world's complexity the simplicity of a single idea may provide a haven from division and enmity. It has been said that all heresies are ultimately errors about Christ, making Him into either an inspired moral teacher, a human being who achieves a purely metaphorical apotheosis, or a divine ghost talking from behind that unfortunate necessity we call the flesh. In either case, there is no reconciliation between Creator and fallen creation — God and man, flesh and spirit, remain apart, alien to each other.

But the Church has always resisted the plausibility and apparent rationality of heresy and proclaimed the infinitely

5

richer mystery of paradox. Paradox, by definition, does not resolve the polarities of our existence into a false simplicity, but holds them in a fruitful tension. Christ is God and man, the infinite contained within the finite, the omnipotent accepting the helplessness of infant, slave, and criminal. This is the deeper, more challenging wisdom to which Donald DeMarco subscribes. And it should be no surprise that his intellectual masters — St. Thomas Aquinas, G.K. Chesterton, C.S. Lewis, Malcolm Muggeridge — have boldly asserted the paradoxes of the faith. In this they follow in the footsteps of the Teacher, whose use of paradox is evident in parables, prophecies, and Beatitudes.

DeMarco's refusal to oversimplify accounts both for the style and form of this book. Though he is a philosopher, he writes with a degree of grace and wit which few philosophers achieve. Like Lewis and Chesterton, he knows how to incarnate his ideas in concrete images and illuminating stories. *The Incarnation in a Divided World* is not a treatise, but a series of interconnected meditations, combining philosophy, cultural criticism, history, apologetics, and the factual clarity of journalism. In short, DeMarco's style defies categories. The result is refreshing, even revelatory.

The thesis pursued in the following pages — that today we suffer from an injurious separation of soul and body, mind and heart — could not be more relevant to our cultural malaise. On the level of mass culture, the rise of violence in the media and the increasing popularity of horror movies bespeak a condition of dividedness. The need to vicariously experience violent death is now endemic. The violent images on the television and cinema screens act as a drug whereby we stimulate our jaded materialistic sensibilities. For it is at the very moment when the body meets its bloody end that we are briefly shocked into an intuitive awareness that body and soul are being torn apart. Because we have forgotten the truth that man is a composite being, a body/soul unity, we resort to such drugs to jolt ourselves into a feeling that we are still alive.

Even at the highest intellectual levels, the Incarnation has become the focus of the conflict between modern ideologies and the Judeo-Christian heritage. In literary theory, for example, the proponents of "deconstruction" (the dominant school in English departments today) claim that the entire Western tradition of metaphysics is epitomized in the image of the *Logos*, the Word made flesh, because meaning is seen to inhere in language just as God and man become one in the Incarnation. The deconstructionists believe that the *Logos* must be destroyed in order for the revolutionary era to begin. One could also point to the pioneering scholarship of Fr. Stanley Jaki in the history and philosophy of science. Fr. Jaki has brilliantly argued that the rise of modern science was in large part possible thanks to the development of Christology in the patristic and medieval eras. Christ, the *Logos*, is the agent of the creation *ex nihilo* and its guarantee of order and coherence. Without the confidence of the knowability of creation, the rise of modern science would not have been possible.

Donald DeMarco is sensitive to all of these intellectual currents, but his strength as writer and philosopher stems from his profound understanding of the intimate and personal dimensions of our life which define our identities in relation to God and to each other. Thus DeMarco writes acutely on love, the family, sexuality, and the degradations of these goods in pornography, abortion, and technologized parenthood. (The chapter on pornography, incidentally, is one of the most incisive treatments of the subject I have read.) He is aware of the way soul and body ought to be nourished and of how they are being starved by the divisions of the modern world. In this sense, if not in strict philosophical terminology, DeMarco is a "personalist," like Pope John Paul II. He never gets lost in theological categories, but remains alive to the psychic and spiritual impact of our cultural crisis.

And despite the fact that much of this book is necessarily taken up with an analysis and critique of decadent institutions and mores, the tone is, in the end, compassionate, open to God's mercy. It is tempting in times like the present to doubt the reality and accessibility of the Incarnation. But this is a temptation that Donald DeMarco refuses. He understands the truth enunciated by the great twentieth century mystic, Adrienne von Speyr: "When one human person kisses another in love he moves toward him, and after the kiss he moves away again. But this moving away is not a removal of love, but the return of the act to the state of love. So it is when the Father sends the Son, who touches mankind in his Incarnation." Above all, Donald DeMarco brings to the contemporary scene the unifying vision expressed by Our Lord at the climax of his high priestly prayer: "May they all be one. Father, may they be one in us, as you are in me and I am in you, so that the world may believe it was you who sent me."

— Gregory Wolfe

Introduction

There is an extraordinary scene in Goethe's Faust where Dr. Faustus, while in a perplexed state of mind, is endeavoring to translate the opening passage of the Gospel according to St. John. At the very outset of his task, he struggles to achieve the proper rendering of the word *logos*, which the Evangelist tells us "was in the Beginning" and is that "by which all things were made." The learned doctor rejects the orthodox version of the opening passage—"In the Beginning was the *Word*"—because every "word" is the expression of a "thought," which, therefore, must have come first. He then writes: "In the Beginning was the *Thought*." Upon further reflection, however, he dismisses *Thought* since thought itself does not have the capacity to generate the world. Thus, he substitutes *Power*: "In the Beginning was the *Power*." But he also finds this expression to be unsatisfactory, for power is nothing unless it is put forth in a "deed." Finally, he writes: "In the Beginning was the *Act*."

Scholars of this great drama have pointed out that the confused mental state of Dr. Faustus, combined with his rejection of the true meaning of the Joannine Prologue, brought his mind into a fit state for listening to the suggestions of the tempter. It is precisely at this moment in the play that the evil spirit, who has a special antipathy for the words of John, is able to exercise his sinister influence over Dr. Faustus.

But apart from the play, this scene has remarkable application to the perplexed state of mind and the rejection of orthodox religious values that characterize the modern world. To elevate Thought above the Word is to paraphrase the philosophy of René Descartes, who is alternately described as the Father of Modern Philosophy and the Father of Modern Confusion. For Descartes, "I think, therefore I am," introduced a new understanding of man as a "thinking thing" and ascribed to thought an independent reality. By assigning a pre-eminent position to Power, one epitomizes the "Will to Power" philosophy of Friedrich Nietzsche, one of the founders of existentialism. Finally, giving supremacy to Act encapsulates the thought of Karl Marx for whom the fundamental imperative was no longer to understand the world, but to change it.

Descartes, Nietzsche, and Marx are among the most influential of all modern thinkers. But their thought remains irredeemably one-sided. Descartes' "thought" exists independently of body, Nietzsche's "power" operates apart from love, and Marx's "act" proceeds outside the domain of wisdom. Thus, these three immensely influential modern thinkers have programmed an attitude of dividedness that has contributed immeasurably to the present condition of our divided world.

From the one-sided thought-patterns of these three thinkers alone, we can easily perceive a general outline of dividedness ranging across the intellectual, political, moral, and theological frontiers of contemporary culture. We observe freedom without responsibility in educational institutions, sensuality without love in the pornographic industry, and images without substance in the world of advertising. We witness the current enthusiasm for de-biologized parenthood, discarnate humanism, and depersonalized individualism. We note the irony of education as if truth did not matter, economics as if people did not matter, and theology as if the natural law did not matter. We perceive the frustration where the individual is alienated from community, where sex is disassociated from procreation, and the finite is separated from the infinite. We see marriage without intimacy, nature without God, life without meaning. In sum, we find a world that is severely dislocated and profoundly divided, one that cries out for wholeness and redemption.

"The Word became flesh," John's description of Christ, is one of the richest and most paradoxical statements in the Gospel, and has an importance that would be difficult to exaggerate. The translation of *logos* as *Word* represents a synthesis of Greek philosophy, Jewish thought, and Christian revelation. In Hellenistic thinking, *logos* meant divine utterance, emanation, mediation. According to the Old Testament it referred to the Word of God as God's manifestation, the revelation of himself, either in creation, in deeds of power and of grace, or in prophecy. In the New Testament, Christ is the true Word of God existing from eternity, through whom (and not through the law) comes grace and truth. According to John, therefore, the Word is understood as an utterance coming from the Father which so perfectly mirrors and manifests God that it is God, but in the person of Jesus Christ who is a source of grace and truth.

The Word becoming *flesh* was a new and startling notion in respect to Judaism which viewed the Word of God in contrast with the flesh. "Flesh" invariably suggested the transitory, the mortal, and the imperfect. The central mystery of the Word becoming flesh—the Incarnation—is that the eternal Word took on human nature, becoming identifiable with mortal man in everything except sin. The Incarnation, therefore, is a great source of hope for man and a living proof that the apparently incompatible qualities of the eternal and temporal, divine and human, spiritual and corporeal can be united in a single reality. The Incarnation offers the hope that man can rise above his solitary and isolated state and, through Christ, become united with God. In a word, the Incarnation offers redemption.

Concerning the redemptive and unifying significance of the Incarnation, St. Thomas Aquinas writes:

> But the fact that God was willing to unite human nature to Himself personally points out to men with greatest clarity that man can be united to God by intellect, and see Him

immediately. It was, then, most suitable for God to assume human nature to stir up man's hope for beatitude. Hence after the Incarnation of Christ, men began the more to aspire after heavenly beatitude; as He Himself says: "I am come that they may have life and may have it more abundantly" (John 10:10). (*Summa Contra Gentiles* IV, c. 54)

Because the Divine can be united with the human means that the human can be united with the Divine. The Incarnation, therefore, is a most powerful aid for man in helping him believe that his redemption and beatitude are not only possible, but eminently realizable. Moreover, it means that a host of other seemingly incompatible factors can also be united. Among these factors are the following: 1) man and God; 2) nature and grace; 3) faith and reason; 4) image and reality; 5) love and permanence; 6) personality and community; 7) morality and wisdom; 8) authority and liberty; 9) time and eternity; 10) matter and motherhood. These pairings, one by one, are at the center of each of the ten chapters that comprise this book. They are at the very heart of a series of controversies involving such diverse subjects as: 1) love; 2) nature; 3) education; 4) the media; 5) contraception; 6) pornography; 7) technology; 8) vocations; 9) spirituality; 10) motherhood.

The Incarnation is the existential ground, the historical reality which provides us with the hope and the confidence that one can overcome the dividedness that marks the world around us. It opens our eyes so that we see potentials for unity where the world sees only occasions for deeper division; it fills our hearts so that we are eager to make the effort to consolidate, integrate, and heal, while the world remains chained to despair. The embodied Wisdom which is the Incarnation, is the touchstone for our abiding conviction that it is harmonious duality and not alienation and dividedness that characterizes the essential order of things. "The creative Wisdom that is the measure of all reality, in the Truth of which every creature is true, has a name: the

Incarnate Word, the Lord Jesus dead and risen" (Pope John Paul II to the International Congress on Moral Theology, October 4, 1986).

1

Love and the Incarnation

In sixteenth century Turkey, it was customary for an official of high rank—known as a "pasha"—to drop in, unannounced, on a family of humbler social station and demand and receive a meal. The hosts considered it an honor to serve the pasha and did not expect any form of remuneration. But the pashas were not always gratefully disposed toward their lower class benefactors. Indeed, as history records, in some instances the pashas actually charged a "tooth tax" as compensation for the wear and tear on their royal teeth!

Class snobbery is a singularly unattractive posture. This is largely because its scornful visage is only too painfully evident. Children spot it instantly and ridicule it without mercy. Fair-minded people are appalled by its hollow pretense of superiority and denounce it in the strongest terms. G.K. Chesterton deemed it intolerable, a sentiment he made emphatically clear in his work on Charles Dickens when he said of that great social reformer:

> He disliked a certain look on the face of a man when he looks down on another man. And that look on that face is the only thing that we have really to fight between here and the fires of hell.

History offers no end of examples documenting the disdain and even contempt people of rank or achievement have expressed toward their inferiors. In purely secular terms, a person is considered important when he attains a position in life that allows him to avoid associating with members of the lower echelon. By imposing a $25,000 membership fee, a golf club can effectively keep out the riff-raff, and at the same time provide an environment in which VIPs speak only to other VIPs. For certain New Englanders, their status was presumed to be so lofty that no one other than the deity was deemed worthy of their association:

> And this is good old Boston,
>> The home of the bean and the cod,
> Where the Lowells talk to the Cabots
> And the Cabots talk only to God.[1]

And "In Canada," as the saying goes, "there are no classes, only the Masseys and the masses," thus punctuating man's remarkable facility for remaining blissfully ignorant of his own pomposity.

An excessive preoccupation with being more important than others carries with it a serious theological liability, although such a liability is not immediately apparent. The more important a person is, in the estimation of the secular world, the more inaccessible he becomes to ordinary people. As his success level rises, the harder it becomes for these people to reach him, and the fewer telephone calls he is obliged to return. God, according to such reckoning, who is the most important person of all, would be absolutely unreachable by mere mortals, and totally unobligated to return any of their calls, that is, to answer prayers.

By projecting secular success values onto God, we construct a deity who, by our own standards, cannot possibly care about us. When Albert Einstein responded to Rabbi Herbert Goldstein's query, "Do you believe in God?", he said, "I believe in Spinoza's God, who reveals himself in the harmony of all being, not in a God who concerns himself with the fate and actions of men."[2] Similarly, Bertrand Russell criticized Christianity for its "depreciation of intelligence and science."[3] He had no use for a God who affirms littleness and simplicity. "Christ tells us to become as little children," he writes, "but little children cannot understand the differential calculus, or the principles of

LOVE AND THE INCARNATION 17

currency, or the modern methods of combating disease."⁴ Russell believes that a man outgrows his need for religion by dint of sheer intelligence. Human beings are too paltry a lot to warrant divine solicitude. Both Einstein and Russell accept the premise that the higher the level of importance an intelligent being assumes, the less reason he has to concern himself with those beneath him.

Sigmund Freud was so conscious of the differences between people, which he believed to be radical, that he came to the opinion that "not all men are worthy of love."⁵ He remarked that one does "an injustice to its object" by loving the unlovable.⁶ Nietzsche went even further and asserted that "The great majority of men have no right to life, and are only a misfortune to their higher fellows."⁷ The highest of these "higher fellows," or God, therefore, would have to die. "If there were a God," said Nietzsche, "I could not endure not being He." If the value of a being rested in its superiority over others, then God could not be tolerated since He would crush man with an overwhelming inferiority complex. Christianity, therefore, is absurd because it would mean that "God, as god of the sick . . . degenerated into the *contradiction* of life."⁸ Divinity must be aloof and remote. If man judges self-centered pride to be a virtue, he assumes that God must also be proud.

For the secularist who creates God in the image of worldly success, religion becomes plausible only once it is irrelevant, for God is not worthy of his divine status if He involves himself in the mundane affairs of weak and fallible man. But if religion is irrelevant, it is useless and might as well not be. If God is not dead, as far as man is concerned, he might as well be dead.

The Incarnation—God descending into the life of man—is so startling a doctrine that the modern world, given its pride and commitment to success, finds it impossible to understand, let alone believe. For God not only answers our prayers, he makes house-calls. What is missing from the success formula is precisely what is needed to begin making sense of the Incarnation. It is the way love expresses itself when the most conspicuous feature in a relationship is one of inequality. It is *graciousness*, the virtue which allows a lover to overcome the barriers of difference, distance, and distinction so that he can descend to meet his beloved.

The Incarnation, like the Fatherhood of God, begins to take on an identifiable character when we observe the beauty of graciousness as it is expressed in everyday human life. The distinguished psychiatrist Viktor Frankl was once wakened at 3:00 A.M. by a telephone call from a complete stranger. The caller was a distraught woman who spoke incoherently for about twenty minutes about committing suicide. Frankl, though extremely groggy, listened to the woman until she concluded the conversation. Sometime later, the woman met Frankl and thanked him profusely for saving her life. Frankl recalled the telephone incident, but pleaded that he was too sleepy at the time to have told her anything that could possibly have been helpful. The woman heartily agreed, remarking that she could not make head or tail of what he was trying to say. "But," she added, "the very fact that a great man like you would spend twenty minutes on the phone at three o'clock in the morning with a complete stranger like me meant that I must be important in some way, and so I decided to go on living."

Graciousness is nowhere more beautifully expressed than when a superior shows special personal interest in an inferior or a subordinate. Graciousness is the largeness of heart that allows a person, no matter how outstanding he is in a particular field, to remain in touch with the whole of humankind. It prevents him from taking himself so seriously that he forgets everyone else. It allows him to give himself where giving is urgently needed.

"Grace," which is the root of the word "graciousness," is *charis* in Greek, meaning the "release of loveliness." The words "grace" and "gratitude" share the same root in Latin. Graciousness is not complete without gratitude. Gratitude is the acceptance and thanks for a gracious release of loveliness. It complements graciousness and invites its renewed expression. A world without graciousness is also a world without gratitude, for there can be no receiving if there is no giving.

The etymological relationship between love, graciousness, grace, and gratitude is noted by St. Thomas Aquinas:

> According to the common manner of speech, grace is usually taken in three ways: First for anyone's love, as we are accustomed to say that the soldier is in the good graces of the king, i.e., the king looks on him with favor. Secondly, it is taken for any gift freely bestowed, as we are accustomed to say: I do this act of grace. Thirdly, it is taken for the recompense of a gift given *gratis*, inasmuch as we are said to be *grateful* for benefits.[9]

Modern society militates against graciousness by making sharp class distinctions that often alienate people from each other by their wealth, education, social position, occupation, color, religion, age, marital status, and health. Even when graciousness is expressed, it is sometimes mistaken for a "patronizing" or "condescending" attitude. People are often slow to recognize acts of true graciousness; but when they do, they hold them in high regard.

In 1982, when Arthur Rubinstein had but a few months remaining in his long and glorious life that spanned 95 years, he invited a 12-year-old piano wizard by the name of Dmitris Sgouros to play for him at his home in Geneva. The lad, happy to oblige, gave a two-hour performance for his audience of one enraptured listener. Rubinstein had heard much about this young musical marvel from Greece, but had always been suspicious of child prodigies. When the private concert was over, Rubinstein pronounced the boy a better pianist than himself.[10]

This is an extraordinary and beautiful act of graciousness, one which the world deeply treasures: the elderly Rubinstein, considered the last of an era of great romantic pianists, doffing his pride, and saluting the arrival of a new piano virtuoso. It is a great, grand-fatherly gesture from a man facing death to a boy who looks ahead to a long and brilliant career. One can easily imagine this act of graciousness having a salutary effect on the young boy, immunizing him forevermore against the temptation to snobbery.

Graciousness is love's willingness to form an alliance with one's inferiors, not because one is directly conscious of inferiority, but because one forgets his own superiority. It is Glenn Gould, perhaps Canada's greatest musician, singing Wagnerian opera to elephants; or the Boston Celtic's basketball legend, John Havlicek, taking pains to show a retarded child how to execute a free-throw. It is Metropolitan Opera star Beverly Sills communicating to her daughter using the universal sign language for the deaf; or a tearful child seeing to it that his deceased pet turtle receives a proper and dignified burial.

Many fathers of retarded children have expressed a graciousness toward them that is as inspiring as it is loving. General Charles de Gaulle, even when he was preoccupied with political matters of historic and global significance, managed to spend time with his Down's syndrome child, Anne. Playing records, singing to her, even dancing before her, he would bring smiles to her face and joy to her heart.[11] The distinguished journalist and TV news commentator George Will speaks lovingly about his "handicapped" son: "Jonathan Will, 10, fourth-grader and Oriole fan (and the best Wiffle-ball hitter in southern Maryland), has Down's syndrome. He does not "suffer from" (as newspapers are wont to say) Down's syndrome. He suffers from nothing except anxiety about the Oriole's lousy start."[12] Sir William Liley, the father of fetology, was so graciously disposed toward retarded children that he adopted one, but not before he had been assured that neither his wife nor any of their five children had any objections.

Harley Smyth is one of Canada's most respected neurosurgeons. After his daughter Anna was born, some doctors suggested that he institutionalize her at three, when she would become entitled to free care. The idea astonished Dr. Smyth and prompted him to ask: "In the elimination of the obvious heartache involved in the receiving of a mentally retarded child into the family of man, what *else* might we eliminate?"[13] In due time, fate (or Providence) answered this question for Harley Smyth in a most dramatic and personal way, for the "something else" that might have been eliminated was his very own life. He was fond of taking Anna to an indoor pool for swimming lessons. One day at the pool, his now seven-year-old daughter noticed a freckle on his back that looked different from the others. She noticed it again the next time they went swimming, and said, "Doctor fix it!" Smyth asked a plastic surgeon at the hospital to examine the curious spot. The "freckle" proved to be a malignant melanoma, an insidiously dangerous form of skin cancer, but caught by Anna at an early stage. The prognosis is good.[14] Consistent with his graciousness and gratitude, Smyth who is a public advocate for the rights of the unborn, sometimes introduces himself as Anna's dad.

Graciousness is a most admirable quality in a human being. Why would it not be admirable in God? Moreover, God is in a position to express graciousness to its infinite degree since he is infinitely superior to man. Of course, human beings are superior to each other in ways that are relatively insignificant. The difference between the most intelligent person in the world and the one who is least intellectually endowed is rather small compared with the former's intelligence and that of God. Moreover, one person is superior to another in one way, but inferior to him in another. Einstein was certainly inferior to Babe Ruth when it came to hitting a curve ball; and for bearing children, the Bambino was no match for his mom. Fundamentally, however, human beings are really more like each other than different. And they are all equally human. This is why graciousness—which is remembering what is more important and ignoring what is less—is an incomparably more human characteristic than arrogance.

In moments when we are not blinded by our pride, we instinctively recognize that love, which unites beings, is incomparably more estimable than pride, which separates them. If God is love, He will be gracious toward even the least of his creatures. Msgr. Robert Hugh Benson once said: "Since God is approaching man, it is not a degradation, but a triumph of his love, that He should come so far down to meet him."[15] The true quality of the Divine is not to be self-contained, but to be self-giving.

Cardinal Ratzinger, in his *Introduction to Christianity*, cites an aphorism that recalls the Christian image of the true greatness of God: *"Non coerceri maximo, contineri a minimo, divinum est"* (Not to be enclosed by the greatest, but to let oneself be encompassed by the smallest—that is divine).[16] To God, who is boundless and infinite, the "greatest" is really too small for Him and therefore He is not contained by it. At the same time, he embraces the "smallest" because nothing is too small for Him. He is neither contained by the "greatest" nor restricted from the "smallest." He manifests His divinity, therefore, by encompassing everything.

The Incarnation is a perfect manifestation of God's divinity, His graciousness, and His love. Through the Incarnation, Christ takes on human flesh, having consented to be conceived in a woman. Thus, He embraces humanness by becoming human. Coventry Patmore has made the remark that Mary is "Our only Saviour from an abstract Christ."[17] Christ is the solid refutation of the god who is self-absorbed and not solicitous of the needs of men. Nonetheless, even in the early days of the Church, this perfect act of divine graciousness provoked strong opposition. Marcion of Pontus, a second century heretic, rebelled against the Incarnation, saying: "A babe wrapped in swaddling clothes is not the kind of a God that I will adore." Similarly, Nestorius, a heretic of the fifth century exclaimed: "I cannot term him God who was two and three months old."

Men are reluctant to accept Christ as their God when they lack the graciousness in themselves to embrace the least of their own. Christianity demands humility and an affection for littleness. "The mark of the Christian," wrote Bishop Sheen, "is the willingness to look for the Divine in the flesh of a babe in a crib, the continuing Christ under the appearance of bread on an altar, and a meditation and a prayer on a string of beads."[18] When Mary was carrying Jesus, she magnified the Lord; the egotist wants to magnify himself. Christianity is frustrating for the egotist because it offers him an antidote at the very moment he expects applause.

People will sometimes use religion, and their association with the Supreme Being, to claim a superiority of their own. Surely a person with religion is a cut above a mere heathen. But Christianity has to do with shepherds who feed their sheep, not flaunt their superiority over them. When a person does come in touch with the life of the Supreme Being, he finds his universe of affection greatly enlarged, so that he is less absorbed in himself and more concerned about others. Even the Pope, as a shepherd of shepherds is really a servant of the servants of God (*Servus servorum Dei*). Running through the Church is an invisible and inverted hierarchy of humility. One of Christ's last acts was to wash the feet of his disciples, after which He instructed them to wash the feet of each other. "For I have given you an example, that as I have done to you, so you also should do."[19]

St. Paul advises each of us to regard one another as our superiors in order to safeguard against the loss of humility. In his letter to the Philippians, he writes:

> Have this mind in you which was also in Christ Jesus, who though he was by nature God, did not consider being equal to God a thing to be clung to, but emptied himself, taking the nature of a slave and being made like unto men. And appearing in the form of man, he humbled himself, becoming obedient to death, even to death on a cross.[20]

Throughout the movie, *The Miracle of Our Lady of Fatima* (1952), virtually everyone in the town reproached the three children for claiming to have seen the Blessed Mother. "I'm sure the Mother of God has more important things to do," came the typical rebuke, "than speak to children." But the essential point, which is just as easily missed in contemporary society, is that nothing is more important for a mother than speaking to her children. What could possibly be these "more important things" which could have occupied Mary's mind and heart?

In eighteenth century France, aristocratic and socially ambitious mothers sent their children off to country wet nurses, thereby liberating themselves so that they might establish salons and invent epigrams.[21] Today's liberated mother fancies she has much more important things to do than to stay home and involve herself in a round of changing diapers, picking up toys, and making meals. "Make policy, not coffee," reads the feminist's liberation button. Inevitably, however, the coffee makers must labor outside the penumbra of respectability.

Christianity entered the world because a woman was willing to make a child the center of her life. Religion must have a descending arc before it can have an upward swing. It is like an inverted rainbow in which the fall precedes the rise. It is not difficult to understand why the ambitious and self-centered are often irreligious. Christianity invites us to lower ourselves so that we can uplift people. This is exactly what God does through the Incarnation. St. Augustine writes:

> The grace of God could not have been more graciously commended to us than thus, that the only Son of God, remaining unchangeable in Himself, should assume humanity, and should give us the hope of His love, by means of the mediation of a human nature, through which we, from the condition of men, might come to Him Who was so far off—the immortal from the mortal; the unchangeable from the changeable; the just from the unjust; the blessed from the wretched.[22]

The graciousness of great men is a reflection of God in their lives. The drowsy parent who walks the baby in the wee hours of the morning, knowing he has a full day of important business ahead, is gently introducing the child to the graciousness of parenthood, as well as the graciousness of God. "Angels can fly," Chesterton quipped, "because they can take themselves lightly."[23]

Love is the great equalizing force in the cosmic scheme of things: it subdues pride, dissolves differences, and restores unity. The creative act, despite the infinite gap that differentiates Creator from creature, is a celebration of equality because it produces through love the very image of itself. Man-as-lovable is an immediate effect of God-as-love. St. Augustine says, "Because You have loved me, You have made me lovable" (*Quia amasti me, fecisti me amabilem*). And according to Aquinas, "every love of God is followed by a good cause in the creature."[24]

We all want to be uplifted. No one wants to be depressed or abandoned. But we can be uplifted only by allowing a power that is in some sense superior to us, to move us. Love obliterates differences, but its graciousness presupposes it. Inequality is necessary for love to be gracious, although inequality is precisely what love seeks to overcome.

The graciousness of love is opposed by egoism, and is in perpetual danger of becoming entangled in and recaptured by it. First, we are reluctant to acknowledge our inferiority. Once we are helped, we are often slow to express our gratitude. And then we are inclined to assume an air of self-sufficiency and resist additional ministrations of love.

In 1863, and while the Civil War was raging, Abraham Lincoln proclaimed a day of "National humiliation, fasting, and prayer"—a governmental act that would seem highly impertinent, if not slightly bizarre, by present standards. On that occasion, the President stated that Americans have received "the choicest Bounties of Heaven." "But we have forgotten God," he added. "We have forgotten the gracious hand which preserved us in peace and multiplied and enriched and strengthened us, and we have vainly imagined, in the deceitfulness of our hearts, that all these blessings were produced by some superior wisdom and virtue of our own. Intoxicated with unbroken success, we have become too self-sufficient to feel the necessity of redeeming and preserving grace, too proud to pray to the God that made us!"[25]

Lincoln was right. If we forget the graciousness of God, we cannot help but be at war with our neighbor. Pride is the refusal to acknowledge the Divine scheme of things, and a blueprint for our own destruction. In the absence of humility, we reject grace and succumb to the force of gravity.

The Incarnation is love expressed through divine graciousness. It is also the perfect embodiment of humility, as well as the perfect antithesis of pride. For Christians, it provides a way in which they can be honored and uplifted and also the means by which they can honor and uplift one another. It is a panegyric to littleness without in the least depreciating the sublime. It combines in a single reality both the lowest and the highest, thereby personifying the very essence of divinity, since for God, the greatest alone is too small, while nothing can be so small as to escape the sunlight of His all-embracing love.

NOTES

[1]John Collins Bossidy (1860-1928), Toast, Holy Cross Alumni Dinner, 1910. This bit of doggerel is patterned on a toast given at the twenty-fifth anniversary dinner of the Harvard Class of 1880, by a Westerner:

> Here's to old Massachusetts,
>   The home of the sacred cod,
> Where the Adamses vote for Douglas,
>   And the Cabots walk with God.

[2]Paul A. Schilpp (ed.), *Albert Einstein: Philosopher-Scientist*, Vol. I (New York: Harper & Row, 1959), p. 103.

[3]Bertrand Russell, *Why I Am Not a Christian* (New York: Simon & Schuster, 1967), p. 45.

[4]*Ibid.*

[5]Sigmund Freud, *Civilization and its Discontents* (New York: Norton, 1962), p. 49.

[6]*Ibid.*

[7]Friedrich Nietzsche, *Will to Power.*

[8]Friedrich Nietzsche, *The Antichrist* tr. by W. Kaufmann, in *The Portable Nietzsche* (New York: The Viking Press), pp. 585-6.

[9]St. Thomas Aquinas, *S.T.* I-II, Q. 110, a.l.

[10]*Reader's Digest*, Jan. 1986.

[11]Robert & Suzanne Massie, *Journey* (New York: Knopf, 1973), p. 355.

[12]George Will, "The Killing Will Not Stop," *The Human Life Review*, Vol. VIII, No. 3, Summer 1982, p. 108.

[13]Martin O'Malley, "A Doctor's Dilemma," *Saturday Night*, May 1983, p. 23.

[14]*Ibid.*, p. 29.

[15]Msgr. Robert Hugh Benson, *A City Set on a Hill.*

[16]Joseph Ratzinger, *Introduction to Christianity* (New York: Herder & Herder, 1970), p. 101. The author of the quotation is an unknown young Flemish Jesuit.

[17]Quoted by Fulton J. Sheen in *The World's First Love* (Garden City, NY: Doubleday, 1961), p. 64.

[18]*Ibid.*, p. 181.

[19]John 13:15.

[20]Philippians 2:5-9.

[21]Ellen Wilson, *An Even Dozen* (New York: The Human Life Press, 1981), p. 154.

[22]St. Augustine, *The City of God*, 10, 29.

[23]G.K. Chesterton, *Orthodoxy* (Garden City, NY: Doubleday, 1959), p. 120.

[24]*S.T.* I-II, Q. 110, a.l.

[25]Roy Basler (ed.), *The Collected Works of Abraham Lincoln*, Vol. VI (New Brunswick, NJ: Rutgers University Press, 1953), pp. 155-6.

2

Nature and the Incarnation

R.G. Collingwood, in his book *The Idea Of Nature*,[1] describes three distinct views of nature that have appeared in Western history. In the earliest view, men conceived nature as a living organism. The scientific revolution that began in the sixteenth century provided a second image—nature as a machine. The modern era conceives nature in yet another way, as an evolving process. In the first view, nature is full of life; in the second, it has no life at all. Nonetheless, both these images of nature are relatively clear and fixed, though perhaps too much so. The third image is vague enough to border, at times, on the meaningless.

Each of these three ideas of nature is no doubt a stereotype that is greatly influenced by certain intellectual assumptions of its time. A truer image of nature involves all three of these views. Nature is not alive as living things are alive, but it is a principle of motion and activity. It is not a machine, though its structure is highly organized and provides an appropriate object for scientific inquiry. It is not meaningless in its present form, although it is never at any moment complete. Whenever we deal with the idea of nature, therefore, we must resist submitting to the stereotypical view that is currently in vogue. In this regard, history and tradition may help us to gain a more balanced and complete concept of nature.

The prominence of technology and the influence of evolutionary theories have had a great influence in forming the contemporary view of nature as an evolving process. This view is highly compatible with the belief that nature, including human nature, can be changed or at least steered in a new direction. This belief has a powerful impact on how we view ourselves as human beings. It leads inexorably to a radical dualism that separates our physical nature from our spiritual selves. We no longer regard our physical nature as a permanent and essentially unalterable part of our humanity since, presumably, it can be re-fashioned or re-directed.

The contemporary novelist, Walker Percy, graphically represents this dualism—the split of man into two separate selves—when he remarks:

> For the world is broken, sundered, busted down the middle, self ripped from self and man pasted back together as mythical monster, half angel, half beast, but no man.[2]

In the less robust language of the philosopher, St. Thomas Aquinas also affirms man's body-spirit integrity:

> Man naturally desires his very own salvation; the soul, however, since it is part of the body of man, is not the whole man, and my soul is not I. Whence, although the soul might attain salvation in another life, nevertheless it is not I or some man in particular.[3]

Aquinas is saying that man is a body-soul unity and is not to be identified with a part of himself, either the soul or the body. But much more is implied. In order for the body and soul (or physical nature and spirit) to be capable of the high degree of integration that a substantial unity demands—for man is a substantial unity of body and soul—these two aspects must be well suited or coaptated to each other. In other words, man's body and soul must be made for each other.

Modern philosophy begins with Descartes, who is alternately called the Father of Modern Philosophy and the Father of Modern Confusion. Descartes separated nature from mind (soul) to the point that not only were they not suited to each other, but they were completely alienated from each other. He spiritualized mind and mechanized matter (nature) and then presented to the world a new notion of man—a ghost in a machine. In this new image, this "mythical monster," as Percy describes it, man is flesh-less and nature is merely something to be domesticated.

This Cartesian partition, which reduces nature to a perfect object for mathematical and scientific thought, was, in fact, indispensable for technological progress. As a methodological basis for the exact sciences, it was a pre-requisite. Descartes' error was a philosophical one; he thought that a mere scientific method also expressed the truth of reality and the truth of man. He expanded a methodological principle which is needed for a circumscribed problem into a philosophy with universal claims.

The mathematical knowledge of nature, for Descartes, is not what it really is, namely, a highly theoretical interpretation of phenomena, but the very revelation of the essence of things. Nature is reduced to geometry and meaning to mathematics. For this reason Maritain criticizes the Cartesian approach because "It mechanizes nature, it does violence to it; it annihilates everything which causes things to symbolize with the spirit, to partake of the genius of the Creator, to speak to us. The universe becomes dumb."[4]

The continuing progress of modern technology has widened the gap between nature and mind, body and soul. More and more, people have come to accept nature as something outside of ourselves that science must master. At the same time, contemporary theories of evolution have intensified this view by presenting nature as something that is invariably re-structured and re-directed.

Pascal, a contemporary of Descartes, had anticipated the human implications of a philosophy that alienated man from nature. His famous words: *"Le silence eternel de ces espaces infinis m'effraye"* ("The eternal silence of infinite space frightens me") powerfully express the painful alienation man feels when nature no longer has an identifiable personal meaning for him.

The division of man into units of soul and man, or mind and nature, has been a persistent source of great anxiety for modern man. This painful self-estrangement has been amply represented in poetry, painting, and literature. It is also a recurrent theme in existentialist philosophy. The French existentialist philosopher Jean-Paul Sartre perhaps best exemplifies this division.

Sartre, like Descartes, develops a philosophy in which man and nature stand in complete opposition to each other. He calls man a "being-for-itself" and identifies his essential meaning with freedom. In contrast, there is "being-in-itself," characterized by being complete, fixed, unfree, and unconscious. Nature is a "being-in-itself" and Sartre often describes it by images of softness, stickiness, viscosity, corpulence, flabbiness, bloatedness. In a famous passage in his novel, *Nausea*, Roquentin experiences the reality of "being-in-itself" while looking at a chestnut tree in a provincial park; it is an experience of utter disgust as if the objects perceived were inherently nauseating. Philosopher William Barrett remarks that "Behind all Sartre's intellectual dialect we perceive that the In-itself is for him the archetype of nature: excessive, fruitful, blooming nature—the woman, the female."[5]

Sartre himself describes nature as a meaningless and gratuitous paste that inhibits and suffocates him. Far from being at home in nature, he reacts to it and protests its very presence; he finds it overwhelming, nauseating. He writes:

> If man is terrified at the bosom of nature, it is because he feels trapped in a huge amorphous and gratuitous existence which penetrates him completely with its gratuitousness: he has no place anywhere, he is just put on earth, aimless,

without any reason to be there, like a briarbush or a clump of grass.[6]

Because man's meaning, for Sartre, lies in his freedom, he is opposed to anything that opposes freedom. He uses the word "facticity" to designate particular obstacles which freedom has to face. These obstacles are: my *place*, my *past*, my *surroundings*, my *fellow-brethren*, my *death*.[7] Sartre states that it is impossible for us to grasp facticity in its "brute nudity"; we always have the feeling of its complete gratuity, its being there "*for nothing*, as being *de trop*" (excessive, nauseating).[8]

By making freedom absolute, as Sartre does, nature, being a limiting factor, is inevitably viewed as standing in the way of man's destiny. Sartre is very much a man of his time. He is well aware of the contemporary rift between man and nature. But this rift would not be as acute and widespread as it is if it were not for the Cartesian partition and the great technological progress that develops from it.[9]

Psychiatrist Karl Stern develops the thesis in this remarkable book, *The Flight From Woman*, that a rejection of nature is often rooted in a rejection of woman (the "eternal feminine") or more particularly, mother. He mounts a strong case to show that his thesis well applies to such influential modern thinkers as Descartes, Sartre, Schopenhauer, Goethe, and others. There is a profound connection in the psychic life of all human beings, according to Stern, between matter (nature) and mother. He points out that in more than one language these words are etymologically related; the Latin word for matter (*materia*) is also the root for the word mother (*mater*). We cannot reject mother or woman without bringing ourselves into conflict with the world of matter and nature that they symbolize. Conversely, our relationship with nature colors our relationship to our fellow men. The present scientific-technological era, with its increasing power over matter, carries with it a great potential for re-shaping our attitude toward woman, toward ourselves, and toward other people in general. "You cannot topple a hierarchic picture of the world in one sphere," Stern points out, "without causing upheaval in another."[10]

Psychotherapist Rollo May espouses a similar view regarding the subtle though intimate connection in man's psyche between nature and woman, and how modern technology can bring us into conflict with them. May refers to the significance on a psychological level of the expression "*mother* nature." "It is not a far cry," he reasons, "from experiencing the achievement of the splitting of the atom as gaining power over the 'eternal feminine.' The atom bomb sets us into conflict with the symbolic mother."[11]

This radical dualism that separates flesh from spirit and alienates man from nature has penetrated the domain of Christian theology where it is now not uncommon for Christian theologians to proffer and approve it in various forms and to varying degrees.

Philosopher Robert Johann has presented a paper to the Catholic Theological Society of America in which he states, in language evocative of Sartrean thinking, that "the importance of natural processes does not lie in their brute facticity."[12] Johann is speaking about contraception and is arguing that contraception can be justified in the interest of enlarging the human dimension of man. Accordingly, man's "intervention in natural processes is always justified when its issue is an enlargement of human meanings and possibilities." Sex, for Johann, belongs to the realm of the natural; it is the brute facticity of biological function. Thus, it is not an inseparable aspect of man's body-soul unity. We can use technology to negate the possibility of procreation, Johann reasons, because natural fertility can be an impediment in the enlargement of the human dimension. It is difficult to see this argument as anything other than an example of radical dualism in which the natural side of man is regarded as less important than the "human" or spiritual side. Given this dualism—in which the structure of sexuality is mere "brute facticity"—it is then permissible to use technology to negate the natural, although it is never permissible to do anything to negate the "human" or "personal."

Moral theologian Charles Curran also employs the expression "brute facticity." He criticizes Ulpian's definition of the natural law, which stresses what is common to all animals including man, for identifying the natural law with "brute natural facticity."[13] Curran believes that Ulpian's definition seems to favor a dichotomy between nature and reason and assigns nature a position of greater and more fundamental importance. He credits Aquinas with trying to modify the "brute facticity"[14] of this definition, but maintains, nevertheless, that Ulpian's concept of the natural law has created problems in the area of marital ethics. In another place, Curran speaks of "the brute facticity of natural processes."[15]

Curran believes that rationality demands that we interfere with the laws of nature so that we might live a more human existence. He therefore criticizes Church teaching on contraception for giving nature too much importance which can sometimes prevent man from attaining greater personal fulfillment. For Curran, then, the Church is guilty of "physicalism," especially in the area of medical morality, since it wants to identify a moral act with the physical structure of that act.[16] Curran finds an opposition between the physical structure of sex and other dimensions of man: the psychological, the personal, the relational, and the transcendent. But in locating this opposition, he inevitably introduces a radical dualism which divides man into two parts and devalues the natural part. It is not the Church that is *physicalistic* as much as it is Curran and his dualistic colleagues that are *angelistic*.

Curran is impressed, if not carried away, by technology's power to transform nature. "Bulldozers change the face of the terrain," he writes, forgetting that earthworms have done far more to change the landscape, or what the shovel, hoe, and horse drawn plow have meant to agrarian societies. He contends that "man before the last few centuries was powerless to bring about any change in nature,"[17] but "contemporary man makes nature conform to him rather than vice-versa."[18] This historical snapshot is as simplistic as it is naive. Curran does not see that the historical difference in man's using nature to conform to his purposes is one of degree and consequently does not occasion a revolution in moral thinking. Man has always used nature and he has always submitted to nature. Curran also ignores the more pertinent fact that man does not merely "make nature conform to him," but is always nature's servant and interpreter. In order to use nature he must first understand and obey her. The sixteenth century philosopher Francis Bacon, at the very dawn of the scientific revolution, knew with superlative insight that "Nature to be commanded must be obeyed."[19]

But more importantly, Curran fails to distinguish nature which is external to man from nature which is an inseparable part of man's nature-spirit unity. The failure to make this critical distinction allows him to treat all nature in the same way. By treating the natural dimension of man as mere nature, that is, something to conquer and conform to the more "human" dimensions of man, he splits man in two so that one part of man is altered for the benefit of the other. C.S. Lewis saw clearly the ominous implications this process held for man:

> The wresting of powers *from* Nature is also the surrendering of things *to* Nature. As long as this process stops short of the final stage we may well hold that the gain outweighs the loss. But as soon as we take the final step of reducing our own species to the level of mere Nature, the whole process is stultified, for this time the being who stood to gain and the being who has been sacrificed are one and the same.[20]

The stars that science reduces to mere nature for the purposes of measurement lose their splendor. The human soul that psychoanalysts reduce to mere nature for the purposes of scientific explanation loses its freedom. Man's body, reduced to a mere natural structure loses its essential affinity with man as a whole and ceases to be the flesh that incarnates man as an embodied person.

In Anthony Kosnid's controversial work on human sexuality, mention is made of the possibility of bodily presence transcending the "facticity of the male-female dichotomy."[21] One is said to experience "existence in a female body structure,"[22] and the sexual impulse is "biologically tied to procreation and a 'given' in each one's existence."[23] There is an elaborate definition of human sexuality which emphasizes personal relationships but omits any reference to procreation.[24] The apparent dualism between nature and person that is manifested throughout the work has prompted William May and John Harvey to draw the following conclusion:

> We believe that the understanding of human sexuality developed by Kosnik and his fellow authors is predicated upon an extremely dualistic conception of the human person, in which the person becomes an experiencing subject and the body becomes purely subpersonal and subhuman—in which the procreative dimension of human sexuality is devalued, becoming merely a biological given, a part of the world of nature, an impersonal "it" over which the experiencing subject has been given full dominion.[25]

The same split is expressed in the writings of Hans Kung. In criticizing *Humanae Vitae* (which upholds the body-spirit unity of man), Kung asserts that in this encyclical "the essential difference between animal-biological and human-responsible is over-looked."[26] What Kung unfortunately overlooks is that it is *man* who procreates, not his animality or biology, just as it is man who thinks, not his brain (man uses his brain in order to think, but it is not his brain that thinks, just as it is not his sex organs that procreate—inasmuch as procreation is a human operation the *whole* person is involved).

Perhaps the clearest manifestation of the radical dualism we are discussing appears in the writings of Joseph Fletcher. He regards physical nature as an impersonal force which is not at all pertinent to our reality as "spiritual beings."[27] Fletcher sees no objection to rearranging human physiology so that the male can get pregnant and deliver a baby. He approves technological interventions that would greatly alter the human anatomy so that man could carry out servile functions more efficiently. His conception of man is essentially Cartesian—a spirit trapped in a cage—with overtones of Sartrean phenomenology:

> Physical nature—the body and its members, our organs and their functions—all of these *things* are a part of "what is over against us,"and if we live by the rules and conditions set in physiology or any other *it* we are not men, we are not *thou*.[28]

What is fundamentally lacking in the thought of these radical dualists is the understanding that man is a unity in multiplicity. Man is not one homogeneous unity or another. He is a composite being. This ought not to be a difficult notion for the Christian mind to grasp; for central to Christianity is the reality of the Incarnation, which not only stands for the indivisible unity of God and man, the Divine and the human, but symbolizes other unities in multiplicity: the two-in-one-flesh of husband and wife, Christ and His Church, the Eucharist, and the Mystical Body. Jesuit scholar Robert Brungs writes:

> The only true Christian unity is unity in multiplicity. From the Holy Trinity (three Persons in one God) through the incarnation (two natures, one Person) to the Church's relation with Christ (Head and members) the only unity is the unity in multiplicity.[29]

Invariably the dualist will disvalue nature for the sake of a more "spiritualized" personality. But this is a false sense of spirituality. We were never meant to be purely spiritual creatures. This is why, as C.S. Lewis has pointed out, God uses material things like water, bread, and wine to put new life into us. God does not think that matter and nature are the least bit unworthy of us. "He invented eating. He likes matter. He invented it."[30] "There's no such thing as *brute* matter," wrote Emile Boutroux, "and that which makes being of matter communicates with that which makes being of spirit."

The Church is repeatedly accused of being "naturalistic" or "physicalistic," when it really grants equal affirmation to both body and soul. Her detractors, in effect, interpret any recognition of the body as a rejection of the soul. But the Church affirms both; she is neither naturalistic or spiritualistic. Similarly, when the Church defends the life of the unborn she is accused of ignoring the pregnant mother. Yet the Church fervently supports the right to life of all human beings.

Gustave Martelet, S.J., uses the expression "conditioned transcendence" to describe the unity in multiplicity that is the human being.[31] Man has a transcendent destiny to develop spiritually as a person, but he attests his intelligence and liberty by respecting his physical nature. Specifically, with respect to sexuality, man perceives a genuine spiritual sense in it when he understands it correctly. The structure of his sexuality is far removed from the category of "brute facticity"; it is an inseparable and inviolable part of him that "conditions" his love. Martelet strongly opposes the notion prevalent among radical dualists that sexuality is human when it unites and simply biological when it procreates. The systematic dissociation of love from life is a denial of man's sexual wholeness, his conditioned transcendence. "It is a fact," Martelet writes, "that the sexuality which gives to love its most original language, does so within the generic context of fecundity which one may call natural to love."[32]

Nature has an inherent affinity with spirit, a fact that escapes the attention of the dualist. As a Scottish philosopher once observed, "nature is not as natural as it looks." The Church has never sought to enclose man in a world of mere nature. Accusations against her of teaching "naturalism" or "physicalism" are entirely without foundation. "The main point of Christianity was this," commented Chesterton, "that Nature is not our mother: Nature is our sister."[33] Nature may have been a solemn word for the naturalists or the evolutionists—for Walt Whitman or for Charles Darwin—but Christianity could always see through her. Christianity has always recognized her diaphanous quality that introduces us to a spiritual realm beyond. She is our sister because we have a common father, an insight Gerard Manley Hopkins beautifully expresses in his phrase: "He fathers-forth whose beauty is past change."[34] We also find this same understanding of nature's affinity with the spiritual realm in the Psalms: "The heavens show forth the glory of God; and the firmament declareth the work of His hands" (Psalm 19).

Man's unity is precarious. It is almost as if a gravitational force were constantly at work pulling him apart, urging and enticing him to divide into elementary, less problematic parts. This instability demands a countervailing force of grace to assist him in achieving the unity in multiplicity which is his wholeness and his destiny.

The integrity of the human being as a body-soul or nature-spirit, undecomposable unity has an important bearing on the subject of grace. If we are separated from our selves through a dissociation from our own nature, we are also separated from a world of grace that flows through nature. Aquinas maintains that "the gifts of grace are joined to nature in such a way that they do not destroy but perfect it."[35] Karl Rahner adds that "the grace of God is permanently in the world in tangible historical form, established in the flesh of Christ as part of the world, of humanity and of its very history."[36] "Nature is the soil of Grace," as Karl Stern reminds us.[37] Grace builds on nature; without nature it is deprived of an important point of entrance in the life of man. For this reason, Chesterton has remarked that without the supernatural what you have left is the unnatural.

The dualists, ironically, over-emphasize the importance of personal relationships, spirit, transcendence, growth, freedom, and so on, out of a genuine concern for man's perfection. Nonetheless, by viewing nature or body as something of an obstacle ("facticity") in the path of man's development, they discourage him from disposing himself to a valuable source of grace which he needs for his perfection. In this regard, they have much in common with Descartes and Sartre who begin their philosophies with consciousness and remain trapped in their subjective centers of consciousness by their very method, which makes it impossible for them to discover that their physical natures are an essential part of their humanness. For Descartes, man is a flesh-less thinking thing; for Sartre, he is existence without an essence. The long shadow of Descartes has not only fallen over atheistic existentialists but over contemporary Christian theologians as well.

Man preserves an important link with God and grace through nature. The more he honors and does justice to his nature, the more he honors and does justice to his Creator. The investiture of grace in the human being is unlike the act of creation which calls beings from nothingness. Grace is produced in something which already exists. Grace is an accident, not a substance. Thus, the affirmation of the whole person—body and soul—best disposes man to receive God's gift of grace.

The relationship between nature and grace has generated many controversies throughout history. Luther believed that man's nature had fallen too far for grace to reach. Concupiscence cannot be conquered, he averred. On the other hand, Rousseau held that man's nature was so good that it did not need grace. He protested that the teaching of original sin was "blasphemy." Both these doctrines—Luther's *corruption of nature* and Rousseau's *innocence of nature*—are false and unchristian.[38] Yet they both affirmed and accepted nature. Neither Luther nor Rousseau wanted to change it: the former because he believed it couldn't be changed, the latter because he believed change was not needed.

The great impediment to grace today lies in a disvaluation of the body. The impressive triumphs in modern technology have convinced many that nature is merely something to be conquered or re-shaped. Man's natural body is therefore regarded as something that can be altered technologically. The justification for this procedure is man's spiritual development which is presumed to be more important than his bodily integrity. Medical technology, which formerly restricted itself to co-operating with nature, is now involved in modifying man's body. But the more we are isolated from our own bodies, the more we lose touch with the world of nature and grace with which we are united through our bodies.

Our deeper need is not for our bodies to be altered by technology, but for our selves to be healed by grace. And the first thing we must do in order to prepare ourselves to receive the grace which is made available to us through the intermediary of nature is to be whole, that is, to be an integrated unity of body and soul, nature and spirit.

NOTES

[1]R.G. Collingwood, *The Idea of Nature* (New York: Oxford University Press, 1960).

[2]Walker Percy, *Love in the Ruins* (New York: Dell Publishing Co., 1972).

[3]St. Thomas Aquinas, *Super primam epistolam ad Corinthios*, XV, lec. ii.

[4]Jacques Maritain, *The Dream of Descartes* (New York: Philosophical Library, 1944), p. 177.

[5]See William Barrett, *Irrational Man* (New York: Doubleday, 1962), p. 254.

[6]Jean-Paul Sartre, *Baudelaire* (Paris: Gallimard, 1947).

[7]Jean-Paul Sartre, *Being and Nothingness*, tr. Hazel Barnes (New York: Citadel, 1964), pp. 457-528.

[8]*Ibid.*, pp. 59-60.

[9]Heidegger uses the word *Faktizität* (factuality) which refers to man's thrownness, being thrown (*Geworfenheit*) into the world. Man's thrownness indicates that man exists without his having chosen either himself or the world. Factuality refers to necessity in traditional philosophy; *existenz*, for Heidegger, refers to that which is free.

[10]Karl Stern, *The Flight From Woman* (New York: Farrar, Straus, & Giroux, 1965), p. 278.

[11]Rollo May, *Love and Will* (New York: Norton, 1969), p. 107.

[12]Robert O. Johann, S.J., "Responsible Parenthood: A Philosophical View," *Proceedings of the Catholic Theological Society of America*, 1965.

[13]Charles E. Curran, *A New Look at Christian Morality* (Notre Dame, IN: Fides, 1970), p. 77. Ulpian (d. 228 A.D.) is a Roman lawyer whose definition of natural law, well known and influential in the Middle Ages, appears, according to Emperor Justinian's *Digest* (or *Pandicts*)—lib. I, tit. ii, I—in Ulpian's *Institutes*. Aquinas refers to Ulpian's famous definition in the *Summa Theologica* (I-II, Q. 94, a. 2). The definition reads: "Natural law is that which nature has taught all animals; this law is not peculiar to the human race, but belongs to all animals." See "The Traditional Concept of Natural Law," *Light on the Natural Law*, Illtud Evans, O.P., ed. (Baltimore: Helicon, 1965), p. 15.

[14]*Ibid.*, p. 79.

[15]Charles E. Curran, ed. "Absolute Norms and Medical Ethics," *Absolutes in Moral Theology?* (Washington-Cleveland: Corpus Books, 1968), p. 123.

[16]Charles E. Curran, *Issues in Sexual and Medical Ethics* (Notre Dame, IN: University of Notre Dame Press, 1978), pp. 40, 68. See also his more recent book: *Moral Theology: A Continuing Journey* (Notre Dame, IN: University of Notre Dame Press, 1982), pp. 119, 144. Philip Keane echoes the same view in *Sexual Morality: A Catholic Perspective* (New York: Paulist Press, 1977), p. 46: "The trend in natural law theorizing among Catholic theologians today is to go beyond physicalism and to try to achieve a larger view of human nature and human persons." The Dutch Dominican Edward Schillebeeckx opposes physical nature with human nature so that in sexuality the nature to be respected is not the reproductive processes but "what is worthy of a human being"—freedom, planning, control of physical nature to serve human nature. *De Linie*, Brussels, Dec. 20, 1963.

[17]Curran, *Issues*, p. 80.

[18]Curran, *Absolutes*, p. 121. See also C. Curran, *Contemporary Problems in Moral Theology* (Notre Dame, IN: University of Notre Dame Press, 1970), p. 113.

[19]Francis Bacon, *New Organon*, Book 1, Aphorism 3.

[20]C.S. Lewis, *The Abolition of Man* (New York: Macmillan, 1965), p. 83.

[21]Anthony Kosnik, ed., *Human Sexuality: New Directions in American Catholic Thought* (New York: Paulist Press, 1977), p. 62.

[22]*Ibid.*, p. 84.

[23]*Ibid.*, pp. 84-5.

[24]*Ibid.*, p. 82.

[25]William May and John Harvey, *On Understanding "Human Sexuality"* (Chicago: Franciscan Herald Press, 1977), p. 15.

[26]Hans Kung, *Infallible? An Inquiry* (Garden City, NY: Doubleday, 1971), p. 36.

[27]Joseph Fletcher, *Moral Responsibility: Situation Ethics at Work* (Philadelphia: Westminster Press, 1967), p. 151.

[28]Joseph Fletcher, *Morals and Medicine* (Boston, 1960), p. 211.

[29]Robert Brungs, S.J., "Biotechnology and Bodiliness," *Communio*, Summer 1981, p. 157.

[30]C.S. Lewis, *Mere Christianity* (London: Fontana, 1961).

[31]Gustave Martelet, S.J., "Morale conjugale et vie chrétienne," *Nouvelle revue theologique* 87 (1965) 245-66.

[32]*Ibid.*, p. 257.

[33]G.K. Chesterton, *Orthodoxy* (Garden City, NY: Doubleday, 1959), p. 112.

[34]*Gerard Manley Hopkins: A Selection of His Poems and Prose* by W.H. Gardner (London: Penguin Books, 1953), p. 31.

[35]St. Thomas Aquinas, *Commentary on Boethius on the Trinity* 2, 3.

[36]Karl Rahner, *The Church and the Sacraments*, tr. W.J. O'Hara (New York: Herder & Herder, 1963), p. 15.

[37]Stern, p. 224.

[38]See Etienne Gilson, *Christianity and Philosophy*, tr. R. McDonald, C.S.B. (New York: Sheed & Ward, 1939), p. xvii.

3

Education and the Incarnation

The greatest need today in Catholic education is the recovery of its proper identity. The two decades that have passed since the Second Vatican Council have witnessed a series of experiments, compromises, and concessions that have plunged Catholic education into a severe identity crisis. This unintended reversal was poignantly described by Cardinal Ratzinger recently when he reaffirmed Pope Paul VI's observation that in the post-conciliar period, Catholics "seemed to pass from self-criticism to self-destruction."[1]

The desire to bring things up-to-date—*aggiornamento*, as the Italians call it—was coupled with an ecumenical interest in building bridges to the world. The more salient results of trying to implement these two concerns, however, were the withering of Catholic ties to its own past and the adaptation of Catholic thought to secular imperatives. No reasonable person could object to the need and propriety of *aggiornamento* and ecumenism, but the historical results show only too clearly that what transpired was a confusion of Catholic identity rather than the successful implementation of these just concerns. The historian James Hitchcock has analyzed how the post-conciliar desire to be fully "relevant" contributed to this confusion and cultivated an attitude that was tantamount to self-negation:

A "relevant" religious education became one in which either Christian doctrines were understood in secular terms or secular ideas dressed up in theological clothing. The notion, which no previous generation of Catholics would have doubted for a moment, that to be a Christian means to see the world in a radically unique way came to smack of narrowness and fanaticism. Catholic doctrines often ceased to be believed because they ceased to be taught, or were taught in such a way that they could not possibly command belief.[2]

Such inordinate preoccupation with the world and the present moment in history inevitably contributed to a severe blurring of the essential meaning of Catholic education. This confusion, however, was the furthest thing from the expressed purpose of Vatican II and the declared intention of its convener, Pope John XXIII. In his opening speech Pope John stated emphatically that his council should uphold orthodoxy. "The greatest concern of the Ecumenical Council is this," he said, "that the sacred deposit of christian doctrine should be guarded and taught efficaciously . . . to transmit that doctrine pure and integral without any attenuation or distortion which throughout twenty centuries, notwithstanding difficulties and contrasts, has become the common patrimony of men."[3]

By abandoning many of the distinguishing characteristics of Catholic education, Catholic schools seemed to have betrayed their distinctive heritage and, to a large extent, lost sight of their very reason for being. This problem is particularly difficult to resolve for Catholics since for them, education is not so much a doctrine or a collection of facts that can be rediscovered and reaffirmed, but a way of looking at things which requires an integration of seemingly disparate elements. In this respect, Cardinal Newman professes that the object of Catholic education "is to reunite things which were in the beginning joined together by God and have been put asunder by man."[4]

In recent years, while the mood was ripe for making concessions to the secular world, many Catholics came to believe that whatever is peculiar to Catholic education might be confined to the sphere of religion or theology. By scrubbing "nonreligious" subjects clean of any Catholic influence, they imagined that they were liberating themselves from a parochial mentality and joining hands with a secular world which viewed the arts and sciences as free from any stain of religion. But this placed too heavy a burden on religion and it soon became apparent that this one subject could not carry the full weight of Catholic education. Some educational leaders, having recognized this very critical problem, sought to unite Catholic education with certain secular forces in order to achieve the double purpose of reinvigorating Catholic thought and at the same time assisting secular society in gaining moral victories in its own political sphere. Unfortunately, this remedy has sometimes had the effect of deepening the dilemma concerning the identity of Catholic education.

At a recent convention in New Orleans of the Leadership Conference of Women Religious, which represents more than 100,000 American Catholic sisters, a resolution was passed that endorsed the boycott of nonunion California table grapes initiated by the United Farm Workers.[5]   Invited to this convention as a featured speaker was one of the 24 nuns who signed the *New York Times* ad on behalf of Catholics for a Free Choice, an organization heavily supported by secular foundations, which holds that direct abortion can be a legitimate Catholic option. The appearance on the program of this nun prompted two archbishops, including the Pope's representative in the United States to cancel their own appearances in protest.

The proceedings of the women's conference indicate that some Catholic leaders find their Church's teaching on abortion—which has been clear and unwavering for nearly two thousand years—to be subject to private interpretation among Catholics, while they find that a political course of action initiated by the United Farm Workers to be a call for the collective and uncritical support of all Catholics. The Catholics for a Free Choice contend that although it is permissible for a woman to expel from her womb a child who is innocent of any wrongdoing, it is intolerable for a Church to expel from its own religious orders unrepentant individuals who are guilty of grossly misrepresenting her teaching. The expressed intention of Vatican II was not that Catholics would receive their mandate from the world for the purpose of changing the Church, but that they would draw from the wealth of resources in their own Church in order to change the world.

Catholic education is crippled once it becomes compartmentalized. If Catholic thought is to be fully alive it must spread throughout the whole academic spectrum. Economics should not be divorced from ethics. Medicine is incomplete without morality. The history of mankind implies a genesis and a destination. Science does suggest the existence of a Creator. And art and literature are impoverished without some reference to a providential order and the transcendental character of beauty.

The purpose of Catholic education is to overcome the bifurcations the world has introduced, to reunite in God the things that God has made. This reunification, however, cannot come about where Catholics are irresolute and indecisive about their own Church teaching and are left vulnerable to the snares and pressures of the world. This reunification can be realized only where it is based on that central fact of history in which God and man are united in the person of Christ through the Incarnation.

The Incarnation is that great and fundamental Christian event which manifests in the form of a personal and existential reality, the unification of opposites. Here, the Word is made flesh, the supernatural fuses with the natural, Church and world unite, and eternity intersects with time. The Incarnation is the touchstone for healing the bifurcations that the world introduces.

These bifurcations which separate elements that should be united with each other have far-reaching implications for education. In the academic domain, they compartmentalize and consequently weaken each discipline. They lead to forms of specialization that insulate each discipline from the others and diminish or even destroy inter-disciplinary communication. They separate *reason* from *faith*, the *natural* from the *supernatural*, the *mind* from the *body*. It is these three bifurcations in particular that we shall examine in some detail for they seem to have played a major role in creating the confusion of identity that plagues Catholic education at the moment.

The Harmony between Faith and Reason

In Vatican II's document on education, entitled the "Declaration on Christian Education," emphasis is placed on "how faith and reason give harmonious witness to the unity of all truth."[6] Also stressed is the harmony and compatibility of intellectual and spiritual values. The presumption of the modern world has been that reason is autonomous and operates most effectively in the absence of faith. Accordingly, faith is regarded as entirely alien to reason and any fusion of the two would represent a contamination of reason, a kind of irrational indulgence in superstition.

But the bifurcation of faith and reason, as well as faith from knowledge, has not led to an age of reason in which the benefits of reason radiate everywhere, but to the dark corner of scepticism. This has also been the case historically. In the sixteenth century, Descartes tried to establish philosophy on the solid and indubitable basis of sheer reason. At the same time, he was attempting to rescue philosophy from the scepticism of Montaigne. Yet his own rationalism led logically and inevitably to a new and more virulent scepticism expressed in the work of the Scottish philosopher David Hume. The same paradoxical development was enunciated by Albert Camus when he remarked that "the philosophy of the age of enlightenment finally led to the Europe of the black-out."

Even so stalwart an intellectual as Albert Einstein understood that reason without faith paralyzes reason. He felt the same astonishment that the ancient Greek philosophers experienced when he exclaimed that the most incomprehensible feature of the physical universe is the fact that it is comprehensible. We cannot reason that the universe must be comprehensible even before we begin to comprehend it. We must have faith that the universe is comprehensible before we try to understand it. "God is not malicious," said Einstein, "nor does he play dice with the world."

This same point about reason's fundamental need for faith was expressed by another twentieth century intellectual giant, Norbert Wiener, the father of cybernetics. Dr. Wiener insisted that "science is impossible without faith."[7] We cannot prove that the mind can grasp the intelligibility of things. We must believe that it can or else we can never get started and remain crippled by scepticism, which is the negation of the mind's proper activity. "Science is a way of life," writes Wiener, "which can flourish only when men are free to have faith."[8]

In the same vein, historians of science have pointed out that science sprang not from Ionian metaphysics, nor from the Brahmin-Buddhist-Taoist East, nor from the Egyptian-Mayan astrological South, but from the heart of the Christian West. And that although Galileo had his personal differences with the Church, he would hardly have taken so much trouble, as one writer explains, "studying Jupiter and dropping objects from towers if the reality and value and order of things had not first been conferred by belief in the Incarnation."[9]

G.K. Chesterton, in his biographical essay on the life and thought of St. Thomas Aquinas, raises the question about whether our primary act of recognizing reality is itself real. Answering for Thomas, he writes:

> The answer is that St. Thomas recognized instantly, what so many modern scientists have begun to suspect rather laboriously; that a man must either answer that question in

the affirmative, or else never answer any question, never ask any question, never even exist intellectually, to answer or to ask.[10]

The pure sceptic, if he did exist as such, would remain quarantined in his own inescapable quandary, not only being uncertain as to whether he can know anything about reality, but remaining hopelessly incapable of even being certain of his own scepticism. Without the fundamental common sense faith in the authority of one's own senses and one's own mind, reason ends before it begins. In his witty and insightful little book, *Escape from Scepticism: Liberal Education as if Truth Mattered*, Christopher Derrick states that the fundamental acceptance of reality, something that cannot possibly be proved by reason, is absolutely necessary if a liberal education is to be at all possible. It is an act which sets the mind free, writes Derrick, "enabling it to start work constructively and in the realistic hope of getting somewhere."[11]

The contemporary mood of scepticism in which truth is considered alien to the human mind leads naturally to a notion of pluralism where everyone's opinion, no matter how deviant from common sense, is counted equal. A *healthy* pluralism, on the other hand, is not founded on scepticism, but a *consensus juris*, as James Madison once expressed it, which is the underlying agreement about justice and right that is needed in order to prevent pluralism from tearing society apart.[12] But the pluralism mounted on the unreliable shoulders of scepticism is a false pluralism and merely a mask for authoritarianism. It is naive in the most pejorative sense of that term to believe that a pluralism in which nothing is held to be true produces a social atmosphere of benevolent neutrality. The opposite is historically the case. Where there is no commonly held standard for what is true or false, each group pushes as hard as it can to advance its own cause. As James Hitchcock has pointed out, "No effective social movement of the past quarter century—the civil rights movement, the peace movement, feminism, environmentalism—has been successful by being voluntarily deferential to other groups."[13]

In absence of a commonly accepted standard, individual groups do their best to make their own views a standard. This is how scepticism necessarily paves the way for authoritarianism and ultimately totalitarianism. The totalitarian state welcomes convictionless people because it can utilize them or reshape them for its own purposes. The social philosopher Hannah Arendt has made the observation that "the aim of totalitarian education has never been to instill convictions but to destroy the capacity to form any."

The contemporary world seeks to divorce faith from reason by making faith private and thereby dismissing it from the public realm. But it does this, not in the interest of erecting a plurality of equally respected views, but in order to establish its own religion. T.S. Eliot warned that the privatization of religion leads to the establishing of a religion by the state:

> the assertion that a man's religion is his private affair, that from the point of view of society it is irrelevant, may turn out in the end to lead to a situation very favorable to the establishment of a religion, or a substitute for religion, by the State....[14]

Thus, when religion comes to be more and more an individual matter, when it ceases to inform the whole life; then a vacuum is discovered, and the beliefs in religion will be gradually supplanted by a belief in the State.[15]

At the moment in the United States, considerable energy is expended in the interest of installing secular humanism as the unofficial religion of the nation, a kind of religion by default. Already the United States Supreme Court (in *Torcaso v. Watkins* and *United States v. Seeger*) has agreed that secular humanism is a religion whose adherents have a right to the benefits that accrue to their church affiliation, such as conscientious exemption from military service. At the same time, however, the courts have consistently denied that secular humanism is a religion that is given a favored place in the public schools.

Scepticism in its pure form is exceedingly difficult to maintain in practice. A few years ago, A. Bartlett Giamatti, President of Yale University, took issue with a body of religiously minded people who opposed abortion on the grounds that abortion destroys a human life. Giamatti accused his antagonists of "presuming to say when life begins, which God alone knows." The Yale University president's scepticism applied only to the area of when human life begins, but not to what are the things which only God knows. How does someone other than God know what are the things which God alone knows? A true sceptic would be tongue-tied about God's existence, let alone God's incommunicable thoughts. It would be far easier to ascertain the beginning of human life, than to determine which thoughts God keeps to himself. The message that Giamatti was delivering might appear on the surface to be merely an honest admission of culpable ignorance; but its real point—that it is immoral to oppose abortion—is authoritarian in its core.

To be right and to know one is right may very well be an occasion for pride. Sir Francis Bacon warned in his *Advancement of Learning* that "knowledge has in it somewhat of the serpent and therefore, when it enters into a man it makes him swell. *Scientia inflat.* If taken without the true corrective, it has in itself some nature of venom or malignity and one of that venom is swelling or pride." But the corrective is found in humility, not in a scepticism which keeps a person in a constant state of uncertainty. It is possible to be educated without falling into pride, to attain excellence without the ungainly accompaniment of arrogance. Scepticism is not only an unworthy replacement for humility, but even this unlovely vacancy in the mind is not immune to pride.

According to Thomas Aquinas, "The human intellect is measured by things so that man's thought is not true on its own account but is called true in virtue of its conformity with things."[16] The human being who has a great deal of knowledge, therefore, can find reason for preserving a humble attitude in the fact that the truth of his thought is determined by how well it conforms to something outside of himself.

Many modern thinkers argue that because Catholic education incorporates faith, Catholics are not free to exercise their power of reason. But the reverse is the case. Without a fundamental faith that the world is knowable, a point which man cannot prove, reason remains incapable of making any assertions that have any real validity. By trying to make reason do more than it can, one makes an invalid of it. Faith releases the power of reason, illuminates it, gives it direction. St. Augustine adopted from Isaiah 7:9 the phrase "Unless you will believe, you will not understand," as his working motto. According to the great historian of philosophy, Etienne Gilson, these words are and will always remain the charter of every Christian philosophy. But they were also, in effect, the charter of great scientific thinkers such as Einstein and Wiener. And that great scientific world-shaker, Sir Isaac Newton, was the same man who always carried the Bible under his arm.[17]

Man is not merely a believing being or merely a reasoning being. He is one being in whom faith and reason penetrate each other. As in the Incarnation, man is a unity whose acts of faith and reason flow from the same being and aspire toward the same end where they are perfectly united in truth.

The Unity of Natural and Supernatural

The Vatican II document on Christian Education also stresses the harmony between the natural and the supernatural. It speaks of the "Catholic school . . . educating its students to promote effectively the welfare of the earthly city, [while at the same time] preparing them to serve the advancement of the reign of God."[18]

One of the immediate dangers that arises when the natural is separated from its relationship with the supernatural is a form of specialization in which each discipline is treated as if it were fully autonomous, having no inherent link to an order beyond itself. Cardinal Newman was acutely aware of this danger and warned that "if you begin the mutilation with the divine, you will break up into fragments the whole circle of secular knowledge."

The increased technical organization of modern life over the past few centuries has brought about a greater and greater need for specialization. During this time modern man has devoted himself to the conquest and organization of the world by economic and scientific techniques. This endeavor has placed a strong emphasis on specialization within the field of education, but it has also created an accompanying spiritual vacuum. The widespread synthesis of economic technocracy with political liberalism has caused many to ignore the fact that every civilization from the dawn of history to the present epoch has accepted the existence of a transcendent spiritual order and has prized it as the ultimate source of moral values and of moral law.

The distinguished educator and former President of the United Nation's General Assembly, Charles Malik, stresses the point that although the founding principles of virtually every major university in the Western world were explicitly Christian, these same universities are now, in the main, disseminators of atheism. Malik contends that universities dominate the West as no other institutions do. They have replaced a universal education which incorporates both the natural and the supernatural with narrow specializations such as: naturalism, subjectivism, materialism, technologism, relativism, futurism, immanentism, Marxism, Freudianism, and so on.[19]

Specialization has been severely criticized by a variety of outstanding thinkers. The Spanish existentialist José Ortega y Gasset terms it barbarous, since it encourages the development of what he calls the "learned ignoramus," "the person who is ignorant, not in the fashion of the ignorant man, but with all the petulance of one who is learned in his own special line."[20] The former President of the University of Chicago, Robert Hutchins, complained that one of the unhealthy features of specialization lies in the fact that the narrower the field in which a man must tell the truth, the wider is the area in which he is free to lie. And philosopher Jacques Maritain argues that "The overwhelming cult of specialization dehumanizes man's life."[21]

Specialization, particularly in scientific and technical pursuits, bears a striking resemblance to the specialization found among animals. Each animal evolves along highly specialized lines of development for the purpose of becoming suitably adapted to specific tasks that help to ensure its survival. The rabbit's quickness, the wolf's ferocity, the eagle's keen eyesight, and the bee's colonial instincts are examples of highly developed forms of specialization. The education of the human being, however, is aimed primarily at developing a well-rounded person by supplying him with general and universal knowledge. The bee produces honey, but man's education should be more than merely a program that enables him to make more money. One of the dangers of specialization is the progressive animalization of the human mind and of life. Another danger is to democracy, for how can an individual make sound judgments concerning the good of the people if he can pass judgment only in the narrow field of his own specialized vocational competence?

The bifurcation of the natural and the supernatural creates another major problem in the form of reductionism. With specialization, one knows something about his particular field while remaining ignorant of what he does not know. But with reductionism, one knows something about the natural order while rejecting what he does not know.

An illuminating example of reductionism is found in the thought of Carl Sagan, host of the popular public television series, *Cosmos*. "The cosmos is all that is or was or ever will be," he states. "It is the universe that made us," he continues, and "we are creatures of the cosmos." "Our ancestors worshipped the sun and they were far from foolish. It makes good sense to revere the sun and the stars, because we are their children."[22] Though he would consider himself a bold thinker, Sagan is merely being narrow. He does not consider that the cosmos itself might have a cause. Nor does he bother with the fundamental issue of how an intellectual-spiritual being, such as man—who knows and loves, builds hospitals and cathedrals, composes poetry and music—could be the effect of hydrogen atoms and helium explosions.

To assert confidently that the cosmos is all that ever was is to replace metaphysics with groundless rhetoric. The contingent elements of the cosmos cannot, of themselves, repudiate the existence of factors other than themselves, no more than the analysis of an orphan could rule out the possibility that he had parents. Sagan is reductionistic and ignorant of his own reductionism. He offers us a myriad of fascinating details about the cosmos, for which we are properly grateful, but his general conception of things is lamentably small. For Sagan, life is not a mystery or a miracle, a precious gift or an expression of divine love; it is nothing but a product of the cosmic process.

This same reductionistic philosophy of "nothing but" is also at the heart of the thought of Sigmund Freud. For Freud, God is *nothing but* the father and the Eucharist is *nothing but* cannibalistic oral introjection. In fact, anything of the supernatural order is "nothing but" a manifestation of the natural order. Needless to say, if one denies the very existence of the supernatural order, one must logically argue that all alleged supernatural activities are nothing but manifestations of the natural. Thus, in Freud's truncated perspective, it is perfectly logical for him to identify religion as an obsessive-compulsive neurosis.

The Christian who accepts the Incarnation, and therefore accepts the possibility of the supernatural fusing with the natural sees no essential disharmony between his earthly father and his divine father, or between primitive sacrificial rituals and Holy Communion. He would embrace both orders, noting that "Even in the child's relationship with his father, there is an awakening or a foreshadowing of our relationship with God," or "Even in primitive rituals, there is a prefigurement of the idea of the Eucharist."[23]

The curious and contradictory feature of Freud's thought is that he resorts to the most fanciful forms of mythology in order to deny the existence of the supernatural, a mythology so similar to the Gospel in many respects as to be a kind of unconscious affirmation of the supernatural. Psychiatrist Karl Stern saw in Freud a hidden motive of prophetic fury. According to Stern, Freud's judgment that religion is a collective form of compulsive neurosis is really a perceptive diagnosis of a religion that had become fossilized in legalistic formulas.[24] Freud's judgment applies to the corpse of a religion, however, and not to a religion that is vibrant and vigorous.

A secondary problem associated with reductionism is that of acculturation. If people believe that this world is all there is, they concentrate all their attention on it and try to draw as much happiness from this world as they possibly can. The Marxist ideal, for example, where there is no longer any conflict between man's desires and the requirements of society, presents the hope that this world alone can provide man with his beatitude. As a Christian observer of culture, T.S. Eliot has rejected this ideal of man living in "uncomplicated adjustment to an uncomplicated world"[25] as inherently unrealistic. For Eliot, this utopian hope poses the very real danger of a mass-life that is a sterile petrifaction. Because we are citizens of another kingdom with its own unique demands, says Eliot, we cannot expect to be perfectly happy in this world. As long as we occupy this earth we need some measure of conflict between Church and State to keep us awake and prevent us from lapsing into one realm or the other. He writes:

> We need a church capable of conflict with the State as well
> as of co-operation with it. We need a Church to protect us
> from the State, and to define the limits of our rights,
> responsibilities, and duties of submission in relation to our
> rights, and to our responsibilities and duties to ourselves and
> towards God. And owing to human fallibility, we may
> sometimes need the State to protect us against the Church.
> Too close identification can lead to oppression from which
> there is no escape.[26]

A further danger of any process of acculturation, in which
people bind themselves together in a mass-culture that rejects
the supernatural, is the likelihood of that culture also rejecting
the nourishing springs of its own past. The worship of the
moment, a practice that Maritain has termed "chrono-idolatry," is
a manifestation of the spirit of reductionism on a temporal scale.
An inordinately high estimation of a culture's importance and
historical independence inevitably results in a stultification of
culture. As a protective measure against this regressive process,
C.S. Lewis recommends reading old books. "Keep the clean sea
breeze of the centuries blowing through your mind," he advises.
For G.K. Chesterton, modern man is marooned in the present.
In his opinion, the contemporary rejection of past wisdom is so
complete that it would be fair to say that "The Catholic Church is
the only thing which saves a man from the degrading slavery of
being a child of his age."[27]

An almost religious belief in scientific and technological
progress along with the experience of an accelerated rate of
changing mores and social conditions have led people to the
conclusion that they no longer have any continuity with the past.
Nonetheless, the progress that has transpired has not been in the
spiritual realm, thereby making it difficult for many to exercise
the very spiritual faculties needed in order to assess their age
correctly. The fact that technical progress has clearly out-paced
spiritual progress has created a climate highly conducive to
ignoring the transcendent while embracing what is immanent.

In his book, *The Crisis of Western Education,* Christopher Dawson offers the following assessment:

> a system of education like that of the modern secular state which almost totally ignores the spiritual component in human culture and in the human psyche is a blunder so enormous that no advance in scientific method or educational technique is sufficient to compensate for it. In this respect we are inferior to many far less advanced cultures which have retained their consciousness of a spiritual order, for wherever this consciousness exists the culture still possesses a principle of integration.[28]

George Bernard Shaw's jibe that a Catholic university is a contradiction in terms is a typically modern remark that betrays an ignorance of the integrating character of Catholic education. Through the Incarnation we find the historical and existential integration of the natural with the supernatural, this world and the world hereafter, time and the timeless. A Christian education inspired by these features of the Incarnation offers the needed antidotes to the bifurcations that man has introduced in the form of specialization and reductionism, acculturation and mass-man, and chronoidolatry and immanentism.

The Concord of Mind and Body

The Vatican document on Christian Education encourages teachers to "give witness to Christ, the unique Teacher, by their lives as well as by their teachings."[29] In Christ there is no gap between his life and his teachings. The Word that is made flesh manifests itself to all men according to its intellectual character; at the same time, the life of Christ attests to and confirms the meaning of the Word in the form of His personal example. Not a shadow of conflict nor any suggestion of a rift exists between the Word and Christ's life.

Two principles of fundamental importance are derived from this realization. The first is that Christian ideals are livable; they can be interiorized and put into daily practice. The second is that Christian teaching should always be related to a person's existential life, always concerned with the integration of thought and action, principles and practice, mind and body.

In the third part of his *Summa Theologica*, Thomas Aquinas deals with the question of whether it was fitting that Christ did not commit any of his teaching to writing. Aquinas answers that it was in keeping with his excellence as a teacher to teach in the most excellent manner possible. And this manner consisted in imprinting His doctrine on the hearts of His hearers.[30] St. Thomas notes that Pythagoras and Socrates were teachers of great excellence and were also unwilling to write anything.

Aquinas understood that Christian teaching demanded a high degree of integration, not only between thought and action, but also between the head and the heart. The Canadian communication theorist, Marshall McLuhan, a deeply committed Catholic in his own right, virtually made a career out of exploring the implications that print had on separating the word from life and the head from the heart. In one of his early works, *The Gutenberg Galaxy*, the book which earned him the appellation, "Oracle of the Electronic Age," McLuhan carefully develops the schizophrenic effect that the print media has had on modern man. "The print-made split between head and heart," he concludes, "is the trauma which affects Europe from Machiavelli till the present."[31]

Schizophrenia may be, as McLuhan argues, a necessary consequence of literacy. But our fragmented modern world is split asunder from a variety of additional forces. Today, most of the information people receive comes not directly from their first hand experience, but indirectly from a variety of other sources. Our education is largely mediated by third parties so that we are often at the mercy of others who often distort what they present for their own private purposes.

Christopher Dawson observes that the artificial character of our modern secularized culture is a "kind of hothouse growth."[32] On the one hand, man is sheltered from the direct impact of reality, while on the other, he is pressured to conform to his particular group. "His whole life," states Dawson, "is spent inside highly organized artificial units—factory, trade union, office, civil service, party—and his success or failure depends on his relations with this organization."

One of the chief reasons liberal society regards censorship as a greater threat to the public welfare than pornography is that in its own fragmented way of viewing things, it does not believe that word can affect deed or that image can influence conduct. Christ taught that a man who had lusted after another man's wife had already committed adultery in his heart. For authentic Christian teaching, thought and action, head and heart are never to be treated as if they were completely independent entities. The fragmented teenager finds it easy to ridicule the Pope, a gesture which the media takes great delight in reporting, because he has been conditioned by culture to disbelieve that doctrine has anything to do with life.

C.S. Lewis, in his science fiction novel, *That Hideous Strength*, presents a character named Mark who displays the kind of personal fragmentation and alienation from life that is prevalent in modern society. "His education," as Lewis explains, "had the curious effect of making things that he read more real to him than things he saw."[33] For Mark, human beings and real events are melted into abstractions. Statistics become the substance as real ditch diggers, ploughmen, and farmers vanish under their cloud. Unconsciously, he avoids using such words as "man" or "woman," preferring to conceal their substantiality under more abstract categories such as "vocational groups," "elements," "classes," and "populations."

Joseph Stalin made the well known remark that the death of one man is a tragedy, but the deaths of a hundred men is merely a statistic. The danger of intellectualization is that the natural relationship between thought and thing can be easily dissolved. Moreover, the intellectualistic language of abstractions, abbreviations, and acronyms is hardly well suited to preserving that power of the word which evokes individual people and unique events. It is precisely this kind of split, which also alienates mind from body and ultimately man from neighbor, that has brought intellectual activity under strong suspicion in the present age. Nonetheless, the mind's intellectual activity need not lose its connection with real being. In fact, in a Catholic frame of reference, the intellect not only remains in touch with its object, but penetrates it so as to reveal even more of its intelligibility.

For Aquinas, it is not abstractions that man knows, although he uses abstractions; it is things that he knows. Moreover, he knows things in their being, not merely in terms of their abstract essences. As a sensible being himself, that is a composite of body and soul, he knows other sensible beings in their existential reality. Knowledge begins by first taking into account the fact that things exist, that is, that they have their own being. Thus, for Aquinas, abstraction is never separated from existence. It always takes place within the apprehended reality of things.

When Igor Stravinsky makes the remark that "To be deprived of art and left alone with philosophy is to be close to Hell," he is treating philosophy as something purely abstract, as an empty thought structure. Art stands for touch and the possession of a sensuous medium. His proximity to Hell is a consequence of thought separated from sensible being or philosophy being devoid of life.

The Platonic philosophy views man as pure reason; the Cartesian philosopher sees him as pure mind. In both cases, man's spiritual activities are completely separated from his body and the physical world. On the other hand, the Catholic philosopher, since he regards man as a composite of body and soul, regards man as a *knower*. A modern commentator of Thomistic philosophy has remarked that "the European man became a thinker after he ruined himself as a knower."[34] As a thinker, man entertains abstractions that are disconnected from real being. But as a knower, he is united with being, intimately involved with what he knows. As a knower, he is always in touch with existence. Knowing is the affirmation of what is, the conformity with truth. Thinking, by contrast, is dis-existentialized knowing. The modern sceptic is a thinker, but not a knower. Similarly, the modern statistician who can count but not comprehend, is merely a thinker. The pure thinker cannot be a lover. Only a knower can be a lover. The root of *caritas* (love) is *caro* (flesh), which is also present in the word "Incarnation." Karl Stern concludes his book on modern psychology, *The Third Revolution*, by reminding us that everything "which is of the psychic order is experienced concretely—not through abstracts, not through apparatuses, graphs, and numbers, but with the stark immediacy of poetic insight. Out of the senses Ultimate Sense arises. Out of the dimness of the flesh (caro) charity (caritas) emerges."[35]

The Catholic educator, then, particularly within philosophy, is eager to restore respectability to intellectual enterprises by reaffirming the mind-body integrity of man and the mind-thing unity of the act of knowing. He stands in sharp contrast with the modern Cartesian dualist who, as a "thinking thing," remains out of touch with a world of real being. He understands that the original Cartesian premise, "Cogito ergo sum," has led to its logical culmination in the unhappy realization that "I cogitate but am not connected."

One of the unfortunate consequences of a distrust in the capability of the intellect to know truth is an immersion into feeling. To a significant extent, the psychology of the individual, with its attendant emphasis on feelings and self-actualization, has supplanted both philosophy and theology, even within Catholic education. But much of the cultural endorsement given to modern psychology is based on the Cartesian assumption that man is primarily a thinker who is alienated from a world he cannot know. Thus alienated, man has only his feelings to serve as a moral compass. Yet feeling cut off from knowledge is just as incompletely human as are empty abstractions. Knowledge alone can be cold and impersonal, but feelings alone are often blind and indiscriminate.

In the legal domain, the Cartesian influence is strongly evidenced in the form of an obsession with privacy. If philosophical judgment is private, then ultimately one's life must also be private. But the private man has little to guide him other than his feelings. William O. Douglas, who served as United States Supreme Court Justice for a record 36 years, cheerfully confessed in his posthumously published memoirs that he decided the Constitution's meaning on the basis of his own "gut reactions." Journalists Woodward and Armstrong point out in their revealing study of the supreme court judges, *The Brethren*, how justice Lewis Powell, Jr., after finding that the Constitution failed to provide a clear basis for a woman's private right to abortion, was prepared to vote his "gut."[36]

The Incarnation as the Word made flesh is a model for Catholic educators to ensure that their intellectual endeavors always remain linked with the vital needs of their fellow human beings. By isolating thought from substance, one runs the risk of a spirit of abstraction which is insensitive to human existence. On the other hand, by isolating existential man from a world of general knowledge, the danger arises that he will immerse himself in the darkness of his own private feelings. Catholic educators should neither be intellectualistic or physicalistic. They should be knowers and lovers of what is.

Albert Einstein once stated that "Everything should be made as simple as possible, but no simpler." The wisdom contained in this epigram is worthy of his genius. Einstein saw something in the pattern of the physical universe that had remained hidden to everyone who preceded him. He saw that the energy locked up inside of atoms could be calculated by multiplying the mass of an object by the square of the speed of light. No one else had ever suspected that mass and the speed of light had anything to do with each other. Sir Isaac Newton's dazzling achievement was to show that by putting mass and acceleration together, one could determine the gravitational force of a physical object. No one would dispute the genius or the realism of these two scientific giants. Moreover, no one would try to split their combinations apart and proceed to argue that energy is just mass or that force is just acceleration. It is the synthesis of apparently disparate elements that is the unquestioned scientific orthodoxy. Things should not be made out to be simpler than they really are.

The Incarnation of Christ represents an insight into the spiritual pattern of the universe. It proclaims to the world that God and man go together in a profoundly intimate way, that eternity and time intersect, and that the Word becomes flesh. This is the Christian orthodoxy; and it is more startling in its originality and more splendid in its implications than any synthesis announced by the world of science. Yet people continue to oppose this Christian orthodoxy in a variety of ways, not so much because they reject Christianity, but because they want things to be simpler than they really are. They want their education to be only reason or only doubt, their science to be just nature or just matter, their morality to be merely abstractions or merely feeling. But things cannot be simpler than they are, not even for God.

The Incarnation stands against the innumerable dichotomies that weaken man and demoralize society. It is our model, *par excellence*, inviting us to do the more difficult things, to resist the alien forces that splinter our lives into meaningless fragments, and to restore our broken humanity to its original unity. Put simply, the Incarnation offers us redemption.

NOTES

[1]Cardinal Joseph Ratzinger Interview (with Vittorio Messori), reprinted in *Fellowship of Catholic Scholars Newsletter*, March 1985, p. 2.

[2]James Hitchcock, *Catholicism and Modernity: Confrontation or Capitulation?* (New York: Seabury, 1979), p. 23.

[3]Quoted by Michael Davies, "Catechetical Revolution—Blessing or Disaster: 1," *Christian Order*, Oct. 1985, p. 485.

[4]John Cardinal Newman, "Intellect, the Instrument of Religious Training," *Sermons Preached on Various Occasions* (London: Burns & Oates, 1881).

[5]"Archbishops cancel appearances at LCWR meet," *Our Sunday Visitor*, Sept. 22, 1985, p. 20.

[6]"Declaration on Christian Education," *The Documents of Vatican II*, W.M. Abbott, S.J., ed., (The America Press, 1968), no. 10, p. 648.

[7]Norbert Wiener, *The Human Use of Human Beings* (New York: Avon Books, 1967), p. 262.

[8]Wiener, pp. 263-4.

[9]Walker Percy, *Lost in the Cosmos: The Last Self-help Book* (New York: Washington Square, 1984), p. 199.

[10]G.K. Chesterton, *Saint Thomas Aquinas: "The Dumb Ox"* (Garden City, NY: Doubleday, 1956), p. 148.

[11]Christopher Derrick, *Escape from Scepticism: Liberal Education as if Truth Mattered* (La Salle, IL: Sherwood Sugden & Co., 1977), pp. 57-8.

[12]Francis Canavan, S.J., "Pluralism & the Limits of Neutrality," *Whose Values*, Carl Horn, ed., (Ann Arbor, MI: Servant Books, 1985), p. 154.

[13]James Hitchcock, "Disentangling the Secular Humanism Debate," *Whose Values*, p. 35.

[14]T.S. Eliot, "The Aims of Education," in *To Criticize the Critic* (London: Faber & Faber, 1965), p. 113.

[15]*Ibid.*, p. 114.

[16]St. Thomas Aquinas, *Summa Theologica*, I-II, 93, 1 ad 3.

[17]Ernest Becker, *The Denial of Death* (New York: The Free Press, 1975), p. 173.

[18]*Op. cit.*, no. 8, p. 646.

[19]Charles Habib Malik, "A Christian Critique of the University," The Pascal Lectures on Christianity at the University of Waterloo, Waterloo, Ont., March 2-3, 1981.

[20]José Ortega y Gasset, *The Revolt of the Masses* (New York: W.W. Norton, 1957), p. 112.

[21]Jacques Maritain, *Education at the Crossroads* (New Haven: Yale University Press, 1949), p. 19.

[22]Quoted in Horn, p. 167.

[23]Karl Stern, *The Third Revolution* (Garden City, NY: Doubleday, 1961), pp. 81-2.

[24]Karl Stern, *Love and Success* (New York: Farrar, Straus & Giroux, 1975), p. 38.

[25]Eliot, p. 27.

[26]Eliot, p. 113.

[27]G.K. Chesterton, *The Catholic Church and Conversion* (New York: Macmillan, 1929), p. 93.

[28]Christopher Dawson, *The Crisis of Western Education* (New York: Sheed & Ward, 1961), pp. 203-4.

[29]No. 8, p. 647.

[30]St. Thomas Aquinas, *S.T.*, III, 42, 4.

[31]Marshall McLuhan, *The Gutenberg Galaxy* (Toronto: University of Toronto Press, 1962), p. 205.

[32]Dawson, p. 173.

[33]C.S. Lewis, *That Hideous Strength* (New York: Macmillan, 1972), p. 87.

[34]Anton Pegis, ed., *Introduction to St. Thomas Aquinas* (New York: Random House, 1948), p. xxiv.

[35]Stern, 1961, p. 199.

[36]Bob Woodward & Scott Armstrong, *The Brethren: Inside the Supreme Court* (New York: Avon, 1981), p. 272.

4

The Media and the Incarnation

In the second of his 1976 London Lectures on Contemporary Christianity, the venerable English author and critic, Malcolm Muggeridge, delivered a remarkable quotation which he attributed to Simone Weil:

> Nothing is so beautiful, nothing is so continually fresh and surprising, so full of sweet and perpetual ecstasy, as the good; no desert is so dreary, monotonous and boring as evil. But with fantasy it's the other way around. Fictional good is boring and flat, while fictional evil is varied, intriguing, attractive and full of charm.[1]

What Simone actually wrote was less arresting and incomparably less lyrical:

> Imaginary evil is romantic and varied; real evil is gloomy, monotonous, barren, boring. Imaginary good is boring; real good is always new, marvelous, intoxicating.[2]

Simone Weil was more interested in communicating pungent ideas than in developing a literary style. Thus, we may forgive Mr. Muggeridge for taking the liberty of embellishing her remark. More important, however, is the notion that a world of images transposes good and evil. This notion is of critical importance since the mass media engulfs the inhabitants of contemporary society with an unceasing deluge of images. Is the media, like the witches in Macbeth, engaged in brewing a devilish potion that makes its imbibers believe that fair is foul and foul is fair? Is the media unconsciously, but inevitably, persuading the masses that good is boring and evil is exciting?

The Bible warns: "Woe to those who call evil good, and good evil, who substitute darkness for light and light for darkness" (Isaiah 5:20). But in the world of the modern media, it is not uncommon for people of celebrity status to defy this admonition. Sting, the name of a rock singer turned film actor, has a positive affection for playing the parts of evil characters. He told his teenage readers in an interview for *Seventeen* (Jan. 1984): "I don't want people to think, 'Oh, he's a good guy.' . . . Bad guys—we're the life and blood and salt of the earth."

The moral implications associated with transposing good into evil and evil into good are naturally quite alarming. The affirmation of such a transposition would be in fundamental agreement with what we might call the "Moral Theology of the Devil." It is the Devil's task to convince people that being is as empty as nonbeing and that nonbeing is as bountiful as being. The Devil wants to get us to act as though the nothingness he holds out for us is infinitely more enchanting and satisfying than the incarnate reality that God has created.

Pure evil, as the Doctors of the Church have ably demonstrated, does not exist. Everything that exists, insofar as it exists. is a reflection of the Creator's goodness, and therefore good in itself. Evil is essentially parasitic; it is the nothingness or the privation that mars something's goodness. Evil is the absence of good that a being needs for its perfection. It is the absence of sight in the eye or love in the heart. For something to be evil it must exist, but be radically wounded.

From a metaphysical point of view, the image is so paltry and tenuous a reality that it exists on the very brink of nothingness. We are speaking here, of course, of fantasy images such as the media produces, and not man who is an image (*imago Dei*) in a substantial and incarnate sense. Because of this close proximity to nothingness, the image is well suited to represent existence in its most wounded form. The image, therefore, substantially impoverished as it is, has a greater metaphysical affinity for evil than for good.

At the same time, it is important to point out that although the fantasy image is greatly handicapped as a vehicle for expressing the ontological richness of being, it can be, in the hands of someone highly gifted, an effective form of artistic expression. Simone Weil maintains that through the power of art, a genius is able to employ images in such a way that he can convince us that good is good and that evil is evil. But genius is rare and takes time. The media makes demands that geniuses could not possibly fulfill. The daily newspaper and the hourly radio and TV programming must, of necessity, recruit people of modest and even mediocre abilities. The problem at hand, however, is not that we have too few artistic geniuses, but that we rely too heavily on the media and too little on life. And as a direct consequence of being so dependent on media images, we run the risk of indoctrinating the masses with the illusion that good is boring and evil is exciting. It is a phenomenon that warrants careful observation. "The Good Newspaper," which was published in Sacramento, California, folded after but 16 months of operation.

The Violent Image

The mad rush to keep the nation supplied with entertaining media images around-the-clock means that the image is usually operating at its lowest level, which is to say at the level of violence. As a mere, threadbare image, we have a form that lies not only on the threshold of nothingness, but occupies a most primitive position on an evolutionary scale of values. The vulgar, artless image is to art as the amoeba is to the chordate or the Neanderthal Man is to the Christian saint. Bereft of any degree of depth, subtlety, or variation, such an image is as limited in its range of expression as Punch and Judy are in the hands of a puppeteer. Violence is primitive and requires nothing more imaginative or sophisticated than the collision of objects. Jon Davison, head of advertising and publicity for New World Pictures, writes:

> Ordinary rape and murder just doesn't make it any more. It's much better to have ultra-violence, chainsaw massacres, x-rated Draculas and continents sinking into the sea with the entire population lost, at the very least.

It is essential to understand that Davison is not merely indulging in hyperbole. The reality is that operating under the added limitations imposed by the lack of time and talent, the image can convey only the most primitive kind of message. The facts bear this out: 8 out of 10 television shows contain violence; an act of violence is shown every sixteen minutes; murder is shown every 31 minutes; and "good guys" are just as violent as "bad guys."[3] In this regard, television programming is analogous to the cartoon where virtually the only marketable relationship that obtains between its characters is one of violence. Indeed, 93.5% of all children's cartoons depict violence.[4] The sole point of the popular "Roadrunner" series is to subject the bedraggled coyote to new heights of surrealistic mega-violence.

A former advertising executive who has abandoned the field to do public service has underscored the severe limitations of television in his book, *Four Arguments for the Elimination of Television.* "The medium is far better suited," he writes, "to conveying such highly visible expressions as hate, fear, jealousy, than showing more 'prosocial' feelings of cooperation, love, and intimacy."[5] The fuzzy imagery of television militates against communicating the more distinctive features of the human being. Morality, grace, love, thoughtfulness, tend to remain amorphous and unfocused. Rough-hewn entities such as sports and violence manage to communicate at least *something*.

Given the inherent limitations of commercial television, a number of inevitable biases arise. Thus, war is better than peace. War is emphatic, has impact and excitement, and is easily focused. Peace, on the other hand, is elusive, diffuse, liquid, and has no visual angle. The hard-edged aggression of the bionic man, for example, is better suited for television than some relatively amorphous Christian who is trying to balance the fundamental paradoxes of life. Likewise, horror is more captivating than beauty and has a decided advantage in market appeal. One commercial ad reads: "Why horror movies are more horrible in the Quintrix color tube." This ad depicts a TV watching family looking horrified. Beauty is tame, vague, and ambiguous.

In addition, death is better than life, lust better than love, competition better than cooperation, and materialism better than spirituality. This transposition of good and evil results chiefly because the meager electronic image does not have the wherewithal to communicate the more subtle spiritual dimensions of incarnate reality. The good that is in reality is too rich and multi-dimensional to be easily reduced to an image. The same cannot be said of evil, which is essentially an impoverished banality. Hannah Arendt was being astute when she subtitled her book about the Holocaust, *Eichmann in Jerusalem*, as "a report on the banality of evil."

The predilection for violence in the motion picture industry is well known. Sylvester Stallone now receives $12 million for playing the part of a grunting muscleman in his Rambo and Rocky series. In 1985 he made $24 million for appearing in *Rambo II* and *Rocky IV* and it is estimated that, given a percentage of the box office take, this figure should swell to at least $40 million.[6] One reviewer trenchantly expressed his disdain for the moral bankruptcy of Stallone's latest film by recording, in box-score fashion: "Rocky IV—Audience 0."

The television soap operas offer further evidence of the affinity the image has with portraying evil. It is axiomatic that a daytime television serial cannot survive if it does not place an unremitting emphasis on immorality. It is now standard fare for a "soap" to feast on such subjects as abortion, incest, infidelity, venereal disease, drug addiction, alcoholism, spouse battering, and murder. A typical synopsis of the week's events of a popular soap opera is described by a daily newspaper as follows:

> ONE LIFE TO LIVE: After bugging Peter's hospital room, Brad discovered Karen and Marco switched Mary with Jenny's deceased child. Bo questioned Asa's new security system at Olympia's crypt, where Pat and Clint snooped. Ted tried to turn Viki against Becky. Wanda filled Clint in on Niki Smith. Marco, who grew more restless, told Karen they would make a nifty couple. Corky, Peter's nurse, made eyes at Brad. Will advised Katrina to work on improving her self-esteem. Marcello drank away his confusion over Katrina and Dorian.

It is not surprising, then, as one survey reveals, that of all sexual encounters on soap operas, only 6% occur between husband and wife.[7]

The wholesale immorality that is portrayed in the "soaps" is of particular interest. The characters are consistently beautiful, often intelligent and talented, and almost always well-to-do individuals who occupy the upper-middle or upper class rungs of the social register. They are not down-trodden, oppressed, or underprivileged people. Fate has been more than kind to them. Ostensibly, they have every reason to be happy with their lot. Nonetheless, they are utterly self-destructive, walking personifications of the seven deadly sins. From an artistic point of view, the extent of their moral turpitude is entirely implausible. The fact of the matter is that goodness makes for tasteless television, whereas licentiousness is the spice that enthralls the viewers and sells the soap.

The media serves a legitimate function in providing people with news, information, entertainment, and recreation. But when it tries to become a substitute for life and a rival to reality, it inevitably inverts moral values, making goodness seem flat and uninteresting, and evil colorful and exciting.

The Image as Reality

Since 1945, 99% of all the homes in the United States have acquired at least one television set. By 1983, according to an A.C. Nielsen survey of viewing trends, daily television watching reached an average of seven hours, two minutes per household.[8] A typical day for an American household now divides into three almost equal parts: eight hours of sleep, seven hours of TV, and nine hours of work or school, including getting there and back. This would seem to leave little time for TV viewers to listen to the radio or read newspapers. However, many people do all three of these things at the same time.

What television does, as well as the images provided by any other electronic medium, is substitute secondary, mediated versions of experience for the direct experience of the world. But when the media assumes a dominant place in people's lives, they may begin to lose their ability to distinguish the image from reality and come to accept images as being reality. Television's Dr. Marcus Welby, a purely fictional character (played by Robert Young), received 250,000 requests for medical advice. When "Julie" of *Days of Our Lives* mulled over an abortion, she was mailed pictures of fetuses.[9] Eileen Fulton, who played the wicked "Lisa" for many years on *As the World Turns*, was punched in front of Manhattan's Lord & Taylor by an irate shopper who had confused the real person with the screen character.

In addition, some people indicate that they actually prefer images to reality. One study had a group of young children asked, "If you had to give up your TV or your father forever, which would you choose? Needless to say, the majority of the little tykes opted to keep the TV and give up Daddy. Another study revealed that many children expressed a preference for media celebrity Burt Reynolds to be their dad, rather than their real father. A heavy number of irate viewers inundated networks with complaints when their favorite soap operas had been pre-empted by coverage of the Challenger shuttle disaster. A feature on the popular game show *Wheel of Fortune* had one contestant declare that she is such a *Fortune* addict that she postponed driving a neighbor to the hospital so she could watch the show. Smiling ruefully, she added: "Unfortunately, the neighbor died. Now *that's* the kind of *Wheel of Fortune* fan I am."[10]

People seem to wonder whether the world is visibly degenerating or is it simply that the news coverage is getting better. Communications experts claim that roughly 85% of our information comes through the media. Given this extraordinarily high dependence on secondary experiences, it is not surprising that many people come to regard the image as the reality. Yet this proclivity to substitute shadow for substance is not particularly modern; rather, it has been an inherent part of the human condition since the dawn of history.

Plato's seventh book of the *Republic* opens with his famous analogy of the cave. Plato asks us to imagine prisoners confined in a darkened enclosure in such a way that they can look only in the direction of an inner wall. On this wall they see mere images, the shadows of life cast by living subjects who traverse a walkway located some distance behind them. These prisoners readily believe that the world of images they observe is real. Moreover, they are not open to the possibility that they may be deceived. Plato states that it would be exceedingly difficult to divert the prisoner-addicts' attention from falsehood to reality.

For Plato, this analogy is a parable on education. The great task of the educator is not to transmit information or be entertaining, or captivating; it is to inspire people to turn away from their illusions and face reality. The educator is trying to do something that is at once difficult and unpopular (perhaps more so today than ever before), although genuinely educational and representing potential good.

In his dialogue, *Gorgias*, Plato offers another analogy to illustrate the difficulty of getting people to do something good. Here Plato describes the predicament of a doctor who is prosecuted by a cook before a jury of children. The unfortunate doctor is accused of harming the children with bitter medicine and even surgery. The cook, on the other hand, has been indulging the children with a variety and abundance of sweets. There is no doubt that the children would condemn the doctor, since their allegiance is to a diet of sweets rather than what is good for them.

No doubt G.K. Chesterton had this idea of Plato in mind when he said in 1932:

> Journalism is a false picture of the world, thrown upon a lighted screen in a darkened room so that the real world is not seen and the unreal world is seen . . . We live under secret government, conducted by a secret process called Publicity.

A study conducted at the Australian National University in Canberra provided evidence that during television watching, the viewer's normal processes of thinking and discernment are reduced to a semi-functional state at best. The research team, led by psychologists Merrelyn and Fred Emery, drew the conclusion that television viewing actually inhibits learning. Its report states that "the individual may be looking at the unexpected or interesting but cannot act upon it in such a way as to complete the purposeful processing gestalt. The continuous fixation of the TV viewer is then not attention but distraction—a form akin to daydreaming, or time out."

Television is like the hypnotist's candle. It fascinates and induces a trancelike state, but, unlike a real object with which one interacts, it does not arouse a person to action. Other studies have shown that children who are watching TV are slower to react than children who are doing something else. It seems that while people are watching TV they are being trained not to react. At the same time, teaching, like life, demands interaction. Thus, many communications experts believe that TV does not educate, but implants.

The Media and the Incarnation

Christ is the Word made flesh. In Christ, God takes on humanity that enables him to be born, dwell among men, suffer, and die. The Incarnate God of Christianity is not in any way abstract or remote; He fishes and breaks bread with men, speaks to the multitudes, and heals people through his living touch. He inscribes his words not in books, but, as Aquinas says, "on the hearts of his hearers." He bestows upon the body and upon physical reality a new dignity, entwining the immutable with the transitory, the eternal with the temporal.

The Incarnation establishes a fountainhead for the Sacramental Life of the Church and for the Mystical Body of Christ. Everything about the Church has its source in what the Incarnation symbolizes: unity, community, and touch. The incarnate realities of bread and wine, rock and water attest symbolically and realistically that God's grace is permanently present in the world in a tangible form.

At the same time, the Incarnation gives us a deeper appreciation of the incarnate realities of the embodied person and the surrounding world of nature. The Incarnation is like the sun glorifying what was formerly a dark landscape. We come to value the landscape all the more because it has been touched by a transforming light. Thus, if we separate ourselves from incarnate reality, we separate ourselves from a world of grace and luminosity. And this separation can easily occur through an excessive attachment to the *discarnate* world of media images. This is why Jacques Ellul states, in his book *The Humiliation of the Word* (1985), that "the triumph of images makes acknowledgment of the Incarnation impossible." The image fosters the impression that there is no inner or hidden reality, that the image is the reality.

Incarnate reality elicits involvement, interaction, growth, care, concern, creativity. In short, it arouses one to life. The discarnate image, by contrast, is naturally less capable of eliciting such responses since it is not of itself an object with which one can become involved. Furthermore, the incarnate world has a depth dimension. Incarnate man has interior richness, a living soul revealing mysteries that are intriguing and inexhaustible. Indeed, the very structure of matter provides physical scientists with internal levels whose analyses are endlessly fascinating.

It is perhaps logical that the media, trading as it does in images, would have a natural antipathy toward religion, especially Catholicism, which centers itself both theologically and philosophically around the Incarnation. Two studies by the research team of Lichter and Rothman offer a statistical corroboration of this point. Its first study, based on interviews with 240 journalists and broadcasters at the most influential media outlets (including the *New York Times, Washington Post, Wall Street Journal, Time, Newsweek,* and *U.S. News & World Report*), revealed that 86% of these people seldom or never attended religious worship. The second study, involving 104 individuals Lichter/Rothman identified as "the cream of television's creative community," showed that the same lack of religious worship applied to 93% of them. Only 12% in each group were "raised Catholic," while 23% in the first and 59% in the second group were "raised Jewish" (2.5% of the American population is Jewish while 22% is Catholic).[11]

It may be that in some inadequately understood sense, media moguls are secretly envious of God's creation. Indeed, the created world is incomparably richer and more glorious than the thin image which totters on the verge of nothingness. C.S. Lewis once said that "lust is more abstract than logic." By this he meant that lust seeks a purely imaginary conjunction of an impossible maleness with an impossible femaleness. Something similar can be said of the media and its image when it seeks a purely fictitious paradise in the conjunction of corporate greed with consumer cupidity: the media is more abstract than the mind.

"All art is religious," as Eric Gill used to say. The best of art uses a finite form to symbolize an infinite reality. The great artists throughout history have been, by and large, religious. The media image, however, does not encourage us to see something deeper than itself. It is opposed to the transcendent, lacks diaphaneity and seeks to enclose us in the material. But such enclosure constitutes a fixation with mere things, a form of idolatry which not only transposes good and evil but leads us down a narrowing corridor toward nothingness.

Chesterton understood this well, which is one reason that he had such great love for incarnate reality and the Incarnate Christ. He knew that the marvelous, inexhaustibly beautiful world of creation was of infinitely greater value than mere images, or fictions, or reflections.

> The modern mystic looked for the post, not outside in the garden, but inside, in the mirror of his own mind. But the mind of the mystic, like a dandy's dressing-room, was entirely made of mirrors. That glass repeated glass like doors opening inwards for ever; till one could hardly see that inmost chamber of unreality where the post made its last appearance.[12]

The dandy's dressing-room brings to mind the triptych mirrors of a fitting-room where people have the experience of seeing their image multiplied and reflected to infinity. But this infinity—Kierkegaard referred to it as *Schlechte unendlichkeit* (bad infinity)—goes nowhere. The television personality is a cousin to Chesterton's dandy. He knows that his image is being multiplied endlessly, wherever there are television sets to pick up the signal. But in the end, the images do not lead to God; they vanish into nothingness at the "inmost chamber of unreality." The light goes out, the memory fades, and nothing is left to enjoy or even to remember. Chesterton had as little interest in mirrors as he had in illusions:

> I am interested in wooden posts, which do startle me like miracles. I am interested in the post that stands waiting outside my door, to hit me over the head, like a giant's club in a fairy-tale. All my mental doors open outwards into a world I have not made. My last door of liberty opens upon a world of sun and solid things, of objective adventures. The post in the garden; the thing I could neither create nor expect; strong plain daylight on stiff upstanding wood: it is the Lord's doing and it is marvellous in our eyes.[13]

The Incarnation of Christianity urges us to go outward to a world of reality, to love others, and to do good. The bulk of media images urges us to do the contrary. We are well advised, then, to follow the suggestion of Malcolm Muggeridge, a man who himself made the long, arduous journey from the media to Christ. He enjoins us "To break out of the fantasy, to rediscover the reality of good and evil, and therefore the order which informs all creation . . . [because] this is the freedom that the Incarnation made available, that the Saints have celebrated and that the Holy Spirit has sanctified."[14]

NOTES

[1]Malcolm Muggeridge, *Christ and the Media* (Grand Rapids, MI: Eerdmans, 1977), p. 46.

[2]Simone Weil, *Gravity and Grace*, tr. Arthur Wills (New York: Octagon Books, 1983), p. 120.

[3]According to Dr. Mike Atkinson, a psychologist at the University of Western Ontario who is doing research in the area of media violence. See Margaret Hoggard, "Are our children being desensitized?" *The B.C. Catholic*, March 9, 1986, p. 12.

[4]*Ibid.*

[5]Jerry Mander, *Four Arguments for the Elimination of Television* (New York: 1978).

[6]John Kiely, "In Hollywood, money still does the talking," *Kitchener-Waterloo Record*, Feb. 1, 1986, p. C1.

[7]Walker Percy, *Lost in the Cosmos: The Last Self-Help Book* (New York: Washington Square Press, 1983), p. 44.

[8]"U.S. homes set a record with seven hours a day of TV," (AP), *K-W Record*, Jan. 25, 1984. The five-hour barrier was broken in 1956, the six-hour viewing fixation came in 1971.

[9]"Sex and Suffering in the Afternoon," *Time*, Jan. 17, 1976, p. 38.

[10]Reported by Bonnie Malleck in *K-W Record*, March 4, 1986, p. C9.

[11]See *NFD* Journal, Nov./Dec. 1984, p. 3.

[12]G.K. Chesterton, *The Coloured Lands* (New York: Sheed & Ward, 1938).

[13]*Ibid.*

[14]Malcolm Muggeridge, *Christ and the Media*, pp. 46-7.

5

Contraception and the Incarnation

From a strictly rational point of view, the Incarnation is a most improbable occurrence. The rational mind revolts at the prospect of such radically distinguishable elements as the divine and the human fusing into a single, unified being. For to be rational is to see each component of reality in its exclusive individuality. Mathematics relates all entities to discrete numbers; physics holds tenaciously to the principle of "impenetrability" which instructs us that no two particles of matter can occupy the same exact space at the same precise moment.

The Incarnation introduces into the world the profoundly startling revelation that two can be one, that the law of impenetrability does not apply to God, and need not be a limitation for Christians and others. It means that difference does not necessarily mean separation, and that the divine and the human interpenetrate one another without either forfeiting its identity. St. John of Damascus, writing in the eighth century, describes this feature of the Incarnation in the following way:

> Moreover, the Word appropriates to Himself the attribute of humanity, for all that pertains to His holy flesh is His, and He imparts to the flesh His own attributes by way of the communication of properties in virtue of the interpenetration of the parts one with the other, and the oneness according to subsistence, and inasmuch as He Who

lived and acted both as God and as Man, taking to Himself either form and holding intercourse with the other form, was one and the same.[1]

The Word becoming flesh defies reason, though it is the central historical fact of the Christian religion. "The Incarnation," as Cardinal Newman, a man not given to hyperbole, tells us, "is the most stupendous event which ever can take place on earth."[2]

In his *Disputation concerning the Union of the Word Incarnate*, Aquinas reflects on the reality of the Incarnation and draws our attention to both its mystery and its meaning:

> Indeed, the Incarnation is a unique union, surpassing every communion known to us. . . . Augustine says about this mystery that, if explanation be sought, let us acknowledge that it is a marvel, and if precedent, then that there was nothing like it before; what God can do let us own we cannot probe, for in such cases the whole reason of the fact lies in the might of the Maker.[3]

The Incarnation conveys to us the message that our destiny is not to remain as solitaries, as private entities, but to fulfill ourselves by uniting our life with the life of another. The Incarnation means that intimacy, the unification of two in one, is a possibility.

But in our divided world, dedicated as it is to absolutizing individualism and protecting it through the institutionalization of privacy, it is the presence of alienation rather than the promise of the Incarnation that is dominant. A cursory examination of present culture reveals a broad spectrum of patterns of alienation. People pass each other on the street or in stores or on campuses. They perceive each other, as testified by the fact that they avoid colliding with one another, but remain enclosed in their own private world. Their relationship with each other is what we might call "civil inattention." In elevators, passengers acknowledge each other, but only so they know where not to look. We might describe this as "polite disregard." Ignoring poverty conditions, although not making them worse, has been identified as "benign neglect." And doing nothing in the interest of preserving the life of a baby who has survived an abortion has been termed "aggressive neglect."[4]

The very structure of airplanes, supermarkets, theaters, and countless other places where people congregate, is designed, usually in the interest of efficiency, to keep face-to-face meetings at a minimum. In such structures, people do not meet as much as merely cross each other's paths. By tacitly agreeing to respect everyone's anonymity, they discover how easy it is to be lonely in a crowd.

Our patterns of alienated living have created the by-stander, the on-looker, and the voyeur, all of whom eschew involvement. As sociologists have repeatedly told us, we are becoming a nation of spectators. A relatively few entertainers and athletes can command inordinately high salaries because the mass media provides them a spotlight and an audience of literally millions of spectators. Hence, many people live vicariously, rather than authentically, alienated from their own being.

So advanced is our acceptance of alienation that many people find natural forms of intimacy incomprehensible. For example, a radical feminist manifesto in defense of abortion reads:

> What the official Church position does not acknowledge is the fundamental difference between a fetus and a woman. If every fertilized egg is a person, then the *woman* is downgraded into a non-person, a mere receptacle or incubator with *fewer* rights than that fertilized egg.

What this manifesto fails to recognize is that the Church acknowledges and accepts the Incarnation. If Christians believe that intimacy between the Word and the flesh is not a threat to the identity of either, how much easier it is for them to believe that neither pregnancy nor marriage pose a threat to anyone's identity. The Christian knows that unions brought about by love are not destructive but fulfilling.

Alienated individualism breeds strange fears. It disposes people to fear that if two human beings get too close to each other, they threaten one another's existence, like two subatomic particles that threaten to annihilate each other if they are brought too close together. Pregnancy does not demand that either the child be non-human or the mother an incubator. The alienated view, because it is excessively fearful of losing individuality, annihilates motherhood (as well as love).

The Incarnation is inseparable from Mary's pregnancy, her intimate and symbiotic union with the child in her womb. No true Christian could possibly believe the Annunciation means either that Mary accepted demotion to an incubator or that she agreed to carry a non-human to term. The intimate relationship that exists during pregnancy between a woman and her child makes motherhood possible. And motherhood is not a negation of womanhood but one of its fulfillments.

Even as apparently intimate an act as sexual intercourse can take place routinely while the partners maintain their alienation from each other. We find this inadvertent confession of alienation described in a letter to Dear Abby:

> I am a twenty-three-year-old liberated woman who has been on the pill for two years. It's getting pretty expensive and I think my boyfriend should share half the cost, but I don't know him well enough to discuss money with him.[5]

The "liberated" woman can communicate with a stranger, Dear Abby, better than she can with her live-in "lover." Moreover, given the order in which she arranges her anxieties, concern for finances is well ahead of whatever concern she may feel for her personal alienation. At any rate, it does not seem to bother her outwardly that her sexual relationship—conjunction without communication—is not freeing her from her private alienation.

"Marriage has God for its Author," Pope Leo XIII once remarked, "and was from the beginning a kind of foreshadowing of the incarnation of His Son."[6] Nonetheless, the modern consciousness sees little connection between the Incarnation where the divine and human become one in the person of Jesus Christ and marriage where husband and wife become united in one flesh. It is not unusual to find strategies for modern marriage which are the perfect embodiments of mutual isolation. One doctor, in his "Personal Marriage Contract" for the modern couple, advises husband and wife to agree to premises that will solidify their individuality without any concern being expressed for their mutuality, how their love for one another will be transforming. A few examples: "I accept my ultimate aloneness and responsibility for myself . . . I will put myself first. By keeping myself full, satisfied and not hungry, I will have an abundance of joy, love and caring to give you. . . . Don't expect me to accept you as you are when you fail to maintain physical attractiveness, and fail to take care of your body. . . . I will not diminish you by thinking of you as 'the wife' or 'the husband.'"[7]

The doctor's prescription is incomparably more severe and dogmatic than the Church's teaching on marriage, *Humanae Vitae* notwithstanding, or that of its most demanding theologian. It presupposes, unrealistically, that two individuals have the capacity to become self-sufficient in their solitude. Even if there were perfect people, they would not make marriage perfect—they would make it superfluous. Moreover, it removes all need for reciprocity and mutuality, and naively assumes that the reason many marriages failed in the past is that the partners were not sufficiently narcissistic, or sufficiently alienated from one another. The doctor's formula is an unconscious acquiescence to cultural individualism and, if followed, would actually prevent marriage. There can be no true marriage without intimacy and only persons, not mere individuals, are capable of being intimate.

As an indication of how deeply imbedded alienation is in our culture, doctors now report that sexual anorexia (the loss of sexual desire) has not only risen sharply in recent years, but is so common that therapists recognize it as a specific problem, quite distinct from impotence or other sexual difficulties. According to Dr. Helen Singer Kaplan, head of the Human Sexuality Program at New York Hospital-Cornell Medical Center, the primary cause of sexual anorexia can be linked to a fear of intimacy. Sexual anorexia, however, is a logical development in a society that shuns intimacy and rejects the Incarnation.

Individualism, alienation, and the fear of intimacy are most congenial to, and well preserved by, contraception. In other words, our culture has conditioned people to accept contraception. It has done this by affirming the principle that man's destiny is achieved through individualism while rejecting the *una caro* intimacy that is possible between persons which is foreshadowed by the Incarnation.

Nonetheless, a conflict exists whenever man's life is at variance with his true destiny. Individualism is not a fulfilling way of life. Inevitably there are signs of discontent with contraception, for man longs to be more than a mere individual; he longs for personal intimacy. Dr. Wanda Poltawska, of the Institute for the Theology of the Family in Krakow, Poland, uses natural family planning as therapy for couples who have become alienated by contraceptive sexual intercourse.[8] Nona Aguilar reports in her book, *No-Pill No-Risk Birth Control*, of couples whose relationships improved once they abandoned contraception and adopted natural family planning. One person spoke for many when she said: "I now know the true meaning of the word 'intimate.'"[9]

It should not be surprising in the least that couples express unhappiness with contraception. Contraception is a negation of both the wholeness of the self and the wholeness of the sex act. Because its purpose is to separate pleasure from procreation it is divisive and consequently opposed to intimacy. It prevents the full gift of self that is needed so that husband and wife can be truly intimate with each other. At best, it is compromised intimacy, saying 'yes' to part of the union, saying 'no' to another part. Thus Masters and Johnson discovered more than two decades ago that the Pill makes sexual response slower or even impossible for some women. In their phrase, it throws a "silken veil" before the final stage of orgasm.

Even a magazine as committed to the sexual revolution and the use of contraception as *Viva* (an offspring of *Penthouse*) freely and fully admitted that the alienating effects of the Pill was causing many people to exhibit neurotic behavior patterns.[10] A twenty-six-year-old newspaper reporter states: "I felt completely cut off from my body." A twenty-four-year-old magazine editor writes: "During the entire time I was on the Pill I was subject to really emotional outbursts. I felt like my body and my emotions were simply out of my control. Also it was as if something was blocking my ability to react to things rationally. I had horrible feelings of paranoia—I thought everyone hated me." And a forty-year-old actress adds:

> Just talking about the Pill depresses me. It took me a long time to connect my being so down with being on the Pill, because that's one thing doctor's don't tell you about. I felt so panicky, so incompetent, so alone—all the things that bother me when I'm depressed, only greatly exaggerated. Never again, not ever again, will I put myself through that.

There are psychiatrists who maintain that suicide from pharmacologically induced depression is the leading cause of Pill deaths. In fact, suicide has been reported to the Federal Drug Administration as a side effect of the Pill.

Secular feminists believed that contraception would liberate them from the chain of unwanted pregnancies. Given the astronomically high rates of abortion and divorce, it is all too painfully clear that contraception has not prevented conception as much as it has prevented intimacy. For many women, as

Germain Greer has pointed out, contraception has left them "in a continuing state of sterility, with their own sex drive dulled and their bodies at the mercy of the man." Thus, their present dilemma: use contraception and succumb to men; don't and succumb to infants. Some have concluded that it is better to avoid sexual relations altogether.[11]

This inability to integrate sex with either men or infants is at root a refusal to be sexual. To be sexual is to have the possibility of overcoming the solitude of the singular self and of sharing one's life in an intimate way with another. Sex means that a human being is not destined to remain imprisoned in his individuality. But to use contraception when having sexual relations is to contradict the aim of sex and throw the partners back into their private worlds from which their sexuality had offered them an avenue of escape. If people want to use sex contraceptively so as to retain their uncompromised individuality, they will be tempted to abandon sex altogether because they will discover that they cannot harmonize sex either with the love of a partner or the blessing of children.

It has been the majority opinion among Catholic moral theologians, as Richard Roach, S.J. has pointed out,[12] that contraceptive sexual intercourse does not consummate a marriage. Contraception prevents the *una caro*, two-in-one-flesh intimacy that is needed in order for marriage to be realized.

Christ spoke of marriage in terms of his mystical union with the Church which is his bride. His union with the Church is so intimate that there can be no accommodation for heresy. Likewise, the union in marriage should be so intimate that there can be no accommodation for contraception. Contraception is to marriage what heresy is to the Church. Husband and wife who avoid intimacy and adopt contraception are very much like the priest who is not intimate with Christ and welcomes heresy.

Intimacy, therefore, is union with integrity. It is the coming together of two parties in such a way that the wholeness thus achieved is a union of all parts. But intimacy does not dissolve the two parties; it allows them to share a common life and fulfill a common destiny. It is very much like the Incarnation: unity with plurality, a covenant without alienation; in short, a "communion of persons."[13]

The Incarnation stands firmly against the various forms of Puritanism, Gnosticism, and Manichaenism that denigrate the body to the point where they can find no place for it in theology. According to Pope John Paul II, the fact that Christian theology considers the body "should not astonish or surprise anyone who is aware of the mystery and reality of the Incarnation." "Through the fact that the Word of God became flesh," the Pontiff goes on to explain, "the body entered theology—that is, the science, the subject of which is divinity, I would say—through the main door. The Incarnation—and the redemption that springs from it—became also the definitive source of the sacramentality of marriage. . . ."[14]

Another example the Church offers of *una caro* intimacy is the Eucharist (which also eludes many people in our alienated culture since they prefer not to recognize what it is and insist that it is only a symbol). The Incarnation helps us to understand not only how the Eucharist is the body and blood of Christ, but also how Christians can be intimate with Christ and Christ with them. St. Hilary writes:

> For if in truth the Word has been made flesh and we in very truth receive the Word made flesh as food from the Lord, are we not bound to believe that He abides in us naturally, Who, born as a man, has assumed the nature of our flesh now inseparable from Himself, and has conjoined the nature of His own flesh to the nature of the eternal Godhead in the sacrament by which His Flesh is communicated to us?[15]

There are two great and primary desires that man has. The first is a desire for intimacy. No one wants to remain walled up in his individuality. Not loving or being loved, what some psychiatrists refer to as "no-relatedness" is a curse and a pathology. Each human being has a profound desire to be known and loved by another—to be intimate with another soul. No one wants to be alone in the universe.

The second great desire is a desire for the infinite. There is no finite possession or being that can fully satisfy the human heart. Our appetite for the good is boundless. Whatever joys we taste always leave us with a desire for more. No one is completely satisfied merely with a finite good or a momentary gratification of desire.

The great and difficult task in life is in balancing these two desires. When people engage in contraceptive sex, they seek to satisfy their desire for the intimate while neglecting their desire for the infinite. The result is that they demand their partner or sex itself to satisfy their longing for the infinite. They make idols of each other and of sex. In seeking the flesh without the Word, they hope to extract the infinite from the finite, an unhappy experience which leads to much frustration and bitter disappointment.

On the other hand, some people seek the infinite without intimacy. They love humanity but not their neighbor, they prefer abstractions to the particular problems that engulf them. They are utopianists or idealists. They search for God but avoid Christ. They seek the Word apart from the flesh.

The Incarnation foreshadows marriage and provides the key to how husband and wife can harmonize the intimate with the infinite. As the Word made flesh, the Incarnation unites the infinite with the finite, the source of Life with particular flesh and blood life. By honoring the unity of sexual intercourse and the openness to life, husband and wife can be intimate with each other while they remain open to God—the Author of Life—and therefore open to the infinite.

Christian marriage offers the most simple and common form by which ordinary people can balance their desires for the intimate and the infinite. But contraceptive intercourse commits a double violence: it prevents intimacy by clinging tenaciously to alienated individualism, and it requires the finite to do the work of the infinite. As a consequence, sex becomes over-rated and then disappointing; marriages fail and new life is looked upon as an accident or burden.

The Incarnation proclaims to married couples that their intimacy should intimate the infinite. That is to say, that by allowing God to have his rightful place in their life, they will reconcile intimacy with the infinite and not seek joy where joy cannot be found.

NOTES

[1]St. John of Damascus, *Exposition of the Orthodox Faith*, 3, 3.

[2]Cardinal Newman, *Present Position of Catholics in England*, 7.

[3]St. Thomas Aquinas, *Disputations concerning the Union of the Word Incarnate*, I.

[4]George Will, "Abortion: The Court's Intellectual Scandal," *The Washington Post*, Sunday, June 19, 1983.

[5]Abigail Van Buren, *The Best of Dear Abby* (New York: Andrews & McMeel, 1981), p. 242.

[6]Pope Leo XIII, *Arcanum Divinae Sapientiae*, Feb. 10, 1880.

[7]John F. Whitaker, M.D., "Personal Marriage Contract," *Woman's Day*, August 7, 1978.

[8]See Fr. Anthony Zimmerman, S.V.D., S.T.D., "Why Marriages Disintegrate When Contraception is Used," *Fidelity*, Feb. 1983.

[9]Nona Aguilar, *No-Pill No-Risk Birth Control* (New York: Rawson & Wade, 1980), p. 102.

[10]Lionel Tiger, "The Emotional Effects of the Pill," *Viva*, Nov. 1973.

[11]*Ibid.*, p. 126.

[12]Richard Roach, S.J., address on sexuality to the Catholic Youth Committee, St. Louis, Oct. 1984.

[13]Pope John Paul II, *Original Unity of Man and Woman* (Boston: Daughters of St. Paul, 1981), pp. 70-77.

[14]*Ibid.*, pp. 175-6.

[15]St. Hilary of Poitiers, *On the Trinity*, 8, 13.

6

Pornography and the Incarnation

Faustus:	Who made thee?
Mephistopheles:	God; as the light makes the shadow.
Faustus:	Is god, then, evil?
Mephistopheles:	God is only light,
	And in the heart of the light no shadow standeth,
	Nor can I dwell within the light of heaven
	Where God is all.
Faustus:	What art thou, Mephistopheles?
Mephistopheles:	I am the price that all things pay for being,
	The shadow on the world thrown by the world
	Standing in its own light, which light God is.

—Dorothy Sayers, *The Devil to Pay*

One cannot see without light. This is as true in the moral sphere as it is in the physical realm. Thus, all moral problems are intimately bound up with the issue of light and darkness. Only light supplies moral illumination. A moral diagnosis cannot take place without it. Darkness cannot free things from their imprisonment in obscurity.

In the moral sphere virtue supplies this light. It provides a perspective of wholeness by which one can see evil comparatively as a deprived condition. In order to see evil as such, one must not be infected by it, for this would impair one's vision. He must

see evil not as a normal property of his own soul, but as
something alien to it. For this reason Plato remarks that a mind
that is or has been evil is not competent to treat anything well.[1]
He points out that evil cannot know virtue and itself, only virtue
can know both itself and evil.[2] And St. Paul tells us that "the
spiritual man judges all things, and he himself is judged by no
man."[3]

Because pornography is extremely pervasive and
influential—an industry that grosses an estimated $10 billion
annually[4]—it constitutes an important mode of informal sex
education. Consequently, many people understand sex in terms
of pornography. Such people do not judge pornography from the
viewpoint of sexual wholeness, but invariably regard it as normal
since it is the only thing they know. Moreover, secular thought
does not view pornography as a privation. Rather, it is willing to
recognize pornography as evil only when a utilitarian calculus has
proven that it is harmful to society. A satisfactory proof of this
sort, however, is exceedingly difficult to furnish. For such
reasons, pornography is a particularly difficult moral problem to
delineate in the present culture.

The Christian, however, should have little difficulty
discerning the evil of pornography. Provided with the
incarnational model of body-soul integrity, and the norms of
sexual wholeness and marital fidelity, the Christian has an
illuminating perspective in which virtue clearly shows
pornography to be a defective and impoverished interpretation of
human sexuality. He sees how pornography denies sex its
transcendent implications, exploits human weakness for financial
gain, and alienates people from one another. He also sees how
pornography demands anonymity, robs sex of its wholeness, and
imposes unrealistic expectations on the sexual partners. In short,
his Christian perspective allows him to diagnose pornographic
man as objectivized, victimized, privatized, depersonalized,
fractionalized, and fictionalized; as deprived of God, rights, love,

name, unity, and joy. Each of these debilitating processes, nonetheless, warrants specific attention and elaboration.

Objectivization—Man Deprived of God

Pornography objectivizes human sexuality. That is, it encloses sex within the material. So circumscribed, sexuality is deprived of any relationship with the transcendent. Pornography, then, is the despiritualization of sex, the attempt to make sex godless. It would, therefore, be as incongruous as it would be unlikely for a pornography parlor to regale itself with stained glass windows.

Educationist David Holbrook, in his anthology entitled *The Case Against Pornography*, develops the thesis that pornography is connected with processes of objectivization associated with modern science. He contends that by objectifying our knowledge of the physical universe, the whole Galilean-Newtonian-Cartesian tradition has reduced nature and man "to the status of dead objects."[5] Galileo claimed that truth lay in the bare mathematical bones of nature—all else was illusion. Yet that 'all else' includes the very roots of our being, and we deny them at our peril. Consequently, Holbrook and his associates interpret the contemporary pornography phenomenon as a sexual imprisonment rather than an emancipation:

> Imprisonment in "objectivity" and "naturalism" is imprisonment in a very limited range of human possibilities—so that the "sexual revolution," rather than representing a "liberation" is actually placing new chains on our intentionality.[6]

The curious attempt to make sexual response an object for scientific observation—something that has much in common with pornography—is directly connected with the belief that the spiritual and relational dimensions of human sexuality are either illusory or non-essential. Masters and Johnson are particularly noteworthy in their obsession with the sheer anatomy and mechanics of sexual pleasure, and their persistent efforts at scientizing sexuality.

Psychiatrist Leslie H. Farber has criticized the Masters and Johnson team for their belief that science will reveal the mystery of sex through the impersonal processes of "abstraction, objectification, and idealization." Rather, as Farber remarks, those who fall prey to such beliefs will be left "to suffer the pathos that follows all such strivings toward heaven on earth."[7] The Russian existentialist Nikolai Berdyaev makes a similar philosophical point when he remarks that in the "objectivized world" people love only the finite and cannot bear the infinite. But, he adds, such preference for the finite enslaves man, whereas the "hidden infinite would be liberation."[8] Hence, pornography, given its objectivized form, is a source of slavery.

But human beings revolt against the various processes that are aimed at their objectivization. "Man," as Paul Tillich has stated, "resists objectification; and if his resistance to it is broken, man himself is broken." Man yearns for something more than what the objective world can provide; and sex is a powerful yearning. He yearns for the infinite. But he also yearns for meaning. Objectification destroys meaning and it is meaning, not mere sensuality, that is essential to sex. Berdyaev reminds us that "to objectify is to destroy meaning; in order to understand meaning one must enter into it, and communion is not objectification."[9]

The desire for sex expresses man's need to find meaning. In the absence of meaning, as Viktor Frankl argues, "when existentialist frustration is most acute, sexual libido becomes rampant."[10] But mere sensuality offers too little for man to overcome the sense of his own "nothingness." After a moment of pleasure, the experience of one's mortality and existential emptiness returns, often with increased intensity. The mere "release" through sensuality, which pornography encourages, does not solve the underlying problem which is a need for meaning.

Objectivizing is an apparent attainment of the transcendent. But since it represents an illusion, it is unrewarding; indeed, it is infinitely frustrating. Pornography is the apotheosis of sensuality. Divinized sex, however, makes a poor god, and offers little nourishment for exiled man. Pornography cannot satisfy man's yearning or his need for meaning; these deeper needs cannot be fulfilled apart from God. With this in mind, Chesterton once made the comment that even the man who knocks on a brothel door is looking for God.

Predictably, the *American Atheist* took strong exception to the Meese Commission's Report that expressed concerns about the dangers of pornography. The President's Commission saw a possible connection between pornography and crime, violence, and child abuse. The *Atheist* was more concerned about the connection between the Commission and censorship (though the Commission did not recommend censorship): "I don't know about the rest of you Atheists out there, but all of this censorship scares me no end."[11]

According to Jon Murray, the *Atheist's* managing editor, religion is the cause of pornography: "When religion dies out, pornography will no longer be necessary."[12] His sympathies are all on the side of pornography ("Pity the poor porno purveyor") and charges that religion is solely responsible for pornography because it tries to suppress human sexuality by suppressing the fact that we are animals: "All religions are based on the supposition of creation and the alleged fact that humans are not part of the other animals on earth."[13]

His charge is a desperate one; for the incarnational Church of Christ has always honored the flesh. Thomas Aquinas, for example, argued that had Adam and Eve not sinned, they would not only have engaged in sexual intercourse, but the delight of sexual pleasure would have been greater in Paradise than it ever could be after the Fall. He reasoned this way because "it is clear that generation by coition is natural to man by reason of his animal life."[14]   Aquinas, as a Doctor of the Church, takes the incarnational view of sex and integrates the spirit and the body. Because the atheist view rejects the transcendent, it finds itself in the embarrassing predicament of objectivizing sex and then indicting Catholics for the resultant pornography on the grounds that they repressed the body, thereby accusing the Church of a fault she had always been wise enough to avoid.

Victimization—Man Deprived of Rights

"She's an ugly cow, but she gives a lot of milk." With such stark imagery, a real estate broker describes the sex business on New York's 42nd Street.[15] The analogy is apt, for what is now a lucrative center for pornography, perversion, and prostitution was, at one time, a cowpath.   More significantly, however, the insinuation is on the mark, that people can easily justify the presence of a moral blight as long as it turns a profit.

Here is a handy formula for victimizing human beings—place money above moral values.   The victims of pornography are all those people whose sexual integrity is considered to be less important than financial gain. 42nd Street is a memorial to human lust and a defeated moral imagination. Public pornography is so unlovely a moral spectacle that it offers a visibly disturbing image, like the picture of Dorian Gray, of moral deformity's inherent ugliness.

"There are people who want to keep our sex instinct inflamed in order to make money out of us," wrote C.S. Lewis. "Because, of course, a man with an obsession is a man who has very little sales-resistance."[16] Thus, one man's lust for the flesh is ruled by another man's greed.   Both are victims, since neither respects the primacy of human values.

The ways in which the pornography empire keeps the sex instinct inflamed are numerous.   Over 200 million issues of more than 800 pornographic magazines are in circulation.[17] The average pornographic film returns about 200 percent on investment in 18 months. One notorious film cost $25,000 to make and has grossed more than $50 million thus far. There are more than 20,000 adult bookstores and movie houses across North America—more than four times the number of McDonald's hamburger outlets. Some of these stores gross more than $10,000 a day. Pornography video cassettes accounted for $360 million in rentals and $40 million in sales in 1984, about one quarter of the video store market.[18] The flow of pornography through cable and satellite transmission is virtually unchecked. Then there are the "novelty" shops with their pornographic paraphernalia of sexual "aids"; the "peep" shows; and even stripping telegrams. And a huge and lucrative business in "dial-a-porn" telephone sex.

The pornography empire has produced a nation of sexual victims. It has also adversely affected marriage and family life. But the saddest class of victims is children. The distinctive difference between conventional pornography and child pornography is that the child victims are always involved against their will. A child is incapable of giving genuine consent to his participation in pornography.[19] At the same time, it is particularly reprehensible for adults to expose children, directly or indirectly, to the virulence of pornography.

Judith A. Reisman directed a Justice Department study of three widely read pornographic magazines. She and her staff analyzed pictures and cartoons involving children that appeared in these publications. They identified 2,016 child-related cartoons, of which 75% involved children in violent or sexual activities. Many of these depict gang rape of child victims, fathers sexually abusing daughters, Santa Claus murdering a child, the Dorothy character of the *Wizard of Oz* sexually involved with her three unusual friends, and so on. Ms. Reisman states, in rather reserved language:

> If some sexual education materials portray children as
> desirable sex partners for adults, this may be of vital interest
> to parents and citizens who are concerned about increases
> in child sexual abuse.[20]

A study by a Toronto psychologist suggests that young people
between the ages of 12 and 17 are the primary consumers of
pornography in Canada and that 37 percent of them watch
sexually explicit videos at least once a month.[21]

An expert witness for the Meese Commission on
Pornography, Victor Cline, a professor of clinical psychology at
the University of Utah, offered some valuable testimony in
explaining how pornography victimizes children in a variety of
roundabout ways. For example, he told how a 13-year-old boy
sexually abused his five-year-old sister over a period of 19
months. The boy was incited to these sexually abusive acts by
reading pornography he had retrieved from a trash dumpster in
his area. Among other casualties of pornography, he discussed a
13-year-old girl and her 14-year-old boy friend who had
discovered her father's secret cache of pornography which
stimulated them to engage in a variety of sexual activities. As a
result, the girl became pregnant. The two young teenagers, prior
to their discovery, were naive and essentially innocent.[22]

Cline also discussed the ill effects of "dial-a-porn" messages
on child callers. The telephone numbers that tap into
pornographic messages are readily available to children.
According to Dr. Cline, "With every child we studied, we found
an addiction effect in making the calls, girls as well as boys." In
several cases, more than 300 calls were made by a particular
child. Parents, especially those who received huge telephone
bills, usually put a swift end to this practice, but there are
instances where the child continues to make dial-a-porn calls
despite strong parental opposition.

People, especially children, have a right not to be unduly
exploited. They also have a right to a form of sex education that
is truly educational and properly moral, rather than the

degenerate alternative that pornography provides. The successful use of sex in advertising should leave no doubt as to how effective sexual images are as a tool for influencing consumer choices. In the hands of skilled pornography merchandisers, this influence is intensified and the harm it brings to an ever widening circle of victims is incomparably more damaging.

Privatization—Man Deprived of Love

The New Woman is a mass circulation magazine that one finds alongside of *Sports Illustrated* and *Better Homes and Gardens* in the periodical section of the local library. A recent issue (August 1986) has a feature entitled "Telephone Sex." The article is a very "discreet" and "tasteful" account of how a very "nice" woman who travels in "polite" social circles earns "good" money at home in her spare time by engaging in "telephone sex" with strangers.

This woman claims expertise at her craft, and gently boasts that many of her clients call her repeatedly, even though the fee for each call is $49. Although she presents a fictitious image of herself over the phone, she feels that she establishes a good rapport with her men. "You're the only woman who has ever really understood me," they say. Some of them insist they have fallen in love with her and express a strong desire to meet her.

But here is where company policy comes to her rescue. She invariably informs her ardent callers, who find that alienated sex leaves too much to be desired, that it is "against company policy" to meet them. In this way she justifies preserving a sexual relationship that demands alienation. She is able to live comfortably and cheerfully with a fundamental human contradiction because it would be against company policy for her to do otherwise.

One of the ironies of "telephone sex" is that it came into being in order to offset the sense of complete human alienation that exists between the voyeur and his pornographic photograph. Pornography demands alienation and estrangement, just as love demands meeting and communion. Love and alienation move in opposite directions. As long as pornography prevails, an authentic interpersonal relationship is precluded. In fact, one of the justifications for pornography is to keep people from breaking out of their fantasies and into reality. "Deny him fantasy and he will be forced to go after the real thing," writes one of its defenders.[23] Needless to say, only in reality can personal love be fulfilled. At the same time, however, we do not want to fantasize about what we should not want to do. Pornography is locked into fantasy. But the real lover wants real union; he cannot be content with a fantasy love that requires alienation.

One pornographer, in attempting to legitimize his activity, described his relationship with the audience in these terms: "They're voyeurs and we're exhibitionists. It's symbiotic."[24] "Symbiotic," however, which denotes a bond serving a common interest in life, is not the right word. The voyeur and the exhibitionist are always at a distance from each other. Meeting is forbidden, let alone bonding. Their collusion offers a kind of confirmation of one another's existence, but each exists impersonally within the other's dream-world.

Pornography is commonly defended on the grounds that it is private, and therefore not the business of the government to regulate. Justice William O. Douglas stated in 1965 when he ruled that married couples should not be restricted from using contraception (*Griswold vs. Connecticut*), that "The First Amendment has a penumbra where privacy is protected from governmental intrusion." This premise was cited again in 1973 to buttress the Court's ruling that abortion is also private. Liberal secular society views contraception, abortion, and pornography as private acts that should not be restricted by the government.

Privacy has been almost an object of veneration in American society ever since Justice Brandeis stated in 1928 that the right to privacy is "the right to be let alone—the most comprehensive of rights, and the most valued by civilized man."

Liberal society, however, neglects a crucial distinction. Some acts are private in the sense that they are not public. Sexual acts have been traditionally considered private in this sense because they are said to be profaned and cheapened when viewed by a third party. At the same time, sexual acts are personal. On the other hand, something is private in the sense that it fails to attain its proper personal realization and is thus *deprived*. It is private in the sense that it is not personal (subpersonal). To treat sex and marriage as private, that is to say, as not being personal, is to treat them in a deprived way. Pornography treats as private something that should be personal. Sex is private in the sense that it is not public, although it is personal. Pornography is private in the sense that it is not personal, although it is public.

It is misguided to defend pornography in the interest of protecting privacy. For pornography does not protect sex from the profaning eyes and ears of the stranger; in fact, pornography assaults privacy and turns sex into a public spectacle. Pornography protects something it should not protect, namely, the arrested development of the person at the stage of being a mere private individual. Sexual morality, however, does protect privacy by keeping it personal and whole, and preventing it from becoming public and impersonal. A human being in his fullness is not private, but personal and social. Pornography attacks the personal privacy that is worth protecting, while promoting a deprived privacy that should be discouraged.

Pornography, then, privatizes man in the sense that it affirms him in his deprived state as a mere individual who is bent on self-gratification. Conversely, it discourages moral privacy which is both a protection against an unwarranted invasion of privacy and an affirmation of the dignity of the person. Hence the liberal contradiction: claims based on the right to privacy provided the legal underpinning for the current sexual permissiveness, yet it is hardly possible to walk by a newsstand, into a corner variety store, or through an airport without having one's sense of privacy rudely assaulted.

There is a subtle but crucial difference between the legitimate right as a person *to be let alone*, and the counterfeit right as an individual *to be left alone*. The former protects our personal privacy, the latter abandons us to our private individuality. By the former, we inhabit civilization; by the latter, we occupy Hell.

This distinction also helps us to disentangle the enigmatic popular expression, "Private Moral Beliefs." A moral belief is private in a psychological sense inasmuch as the individual believer has his own belief. But insofar as moral beliefs are by nature normative and therefore applicable to many persons, they are clearly not private in a moral or personal sense.

"The individual is sovereign," said John Stuart Mill in his 1854 essay, *On Liberty*. Mill's critical error was to mistake the individual for the person. For the individual, everything is private. The person, on the other hand, has a social conscience. Pornography is an affront to persons, though easily tolerated by privatized or deprived persons (better known as isolated individuals). "Man will really be a person," Maritain writes, "insofar as the life of spirit and freedom will dominate in him that of passion and the senses."[25]

Depersonalization—Man Deprived of Name

Leslie Farber and others have criticized pornography for transferring the fig leaf to the face.[26] This insight is a most illuminating one. The face is richly suggestive of personality; the private parts are not. In the words of Nikolai Berdyaev:

> The face of man is the most amazing thing in the life of the world; another world shines out through it. It is the entrance of personality into the world process, with its uniqueness, its singleness, its unrepeatability.[27]

In the human face, two worlds meet. Max Picard, known as the "poet of the human face," says that God enters man's face as a friend enters the house of a friend, without a stir. It is a tempered image, he writes, it is the mildness of God that appears in the face of man.[28]

The face invites meeting and communication. It testifies to one's personal uniqueness. Covering the face and exposing the sex organs symbolizes a repression of personality and its replacement with an impersonal world in which lust is sovereign. The lower appetite needs to be integrated into personality, not separated from it.

Pornography's practice of disdaining the human face has been duly noted. Psychotherapist Rollo May, for example, finds that the Playboy models exhibit a physiognomy which is "detached, mechanical, uninviting, vacuous—the typical schizoid personality in the negative sense of that term."[29] It is exceedingly difficult for the human face to radiate personality if the model's primary function is to serve a pornographic interest. Personality must be primary if sex is to be properly integrated. But if sex is primary, personality becomes suppressed or detached.

Instinctively, we give a person a name. The "name" symbolizes what is singular and spiritual in the person. When love speaks, it speaks the person's name:

> Your name is like a golden bell
> Hung in my heart, and when I think of you,
> I tremble, and the bell swings and rings—
> Roxane! ... Roxane! ... along my veins, Roxane![30]

In the depersonalized, faceless world of pornography, the language of names gives way to a language of numbers. Whenever people are identified by number, rather than by name, there is always a subversion of personality. It happens in prisons, in bureaucracies, in the business world, and in pornography where something called "vital statistics" (36-24-36) is given prominence over a person's name. Names are holy. They signify the whole of one's personality. But numbers render people anonymous. This is why it is so important to remember people's names and to address them accordingly. "Hail Mary" is not merely a salutation, but an affirmation of personality and a recognition of the victory of grace over gravity, of personality over the sinfulness of the world.

The legendary film producer Cecil B. DeMille used to complain that the Hollywood girls who emerged from the love-goddess assembly line all looked alike. "Their faces look like slabs of concrete," he said. "Maybe the average Hollywood glamour girl should be numbered instead of named."[31] Mechanization, which invariably stamps things with sameness, is a logical enemy of personality. Its language is numbers, not names, mathematical symbols, not inimitable faces. The affinity between mechanization and pornography is made apparent by their common language of numbers.

Pornography is obsessed with numbers: the size of organs, the duration of intercourse, the variety of positions, the number of partners, and the frequency of orgasm. But this morbid preoccupation with numbers obscures the world of personality, while establishing in its place, an impersonal world where love is impossible and sex ultimately becomes meaningless.

We are persons, with faces and names. As such, we achieve our health, wholeness and happiness. We rightly feel shame, therefore, when we treat ourselves or when others treat us in ways that are contrary to our personal dignity. Thus, there are two kinds of shame, a *concealing* shame when one tries to hide the fact that one is treating others as sexual objects, and a *protecting* shame when one tries to protect one's sexuality from being regarded as an object by others.[32]

These two shames are relatable to the two notions of privacy as *not personal* and *not public*. Concealing shame urges one to conceal one's having made private (depersonalized) sexual acts that are essentially personal. Protecting shame urges one to protect sexual acts that are private (but personal) from being made public (depersonalized). Pornography preaches that all shame is unnatural. But this premise must affirm a depersonalized world that is dominated by lust. Thus, if shame is unnatural, personal love is impossible.

Shame exists, not because there is something inherently shameful about sex, but because sex is essentially personal and is desecrated when it is depersonalized. Pope John Paul II, in his "Theology of the Body," states that lust

> "depersonalizes" man making him an object "for the other." Instead of being "together with the other"—a subject in unity, in fact, in the sacramental unity "of the body"—man becomes an object for man: the female for the male and vice versa.[33]

It is precisely this awareness that men and women can treat each other as sexual objects that produces shame. The Holy Father goes on to speak of shame as rooted in "alienation" and "detachment from love," conditions which also prevent the establishment of a "communion of persons."[34] Man feels shame because he knows that lust and lovelessness prevent him from realizing his divine calling which is to live by personal love.

The shame that one sex has of the other is overcome positively through personal love, that is through the sublimation of shame, or negatively through depravity and the loss of shame, that is through desublimation.[35] Pornography promotes shame-lessness through desublimation[36] and by the suppression of personality. This is why one critic of pornography asserts that "Pornography doesn't *cause* depravity and corruption, it *is* depravity and corruption."[37]

The Pope has painstakingly explained how the *Genesis* account describes shame as an appropriate experience for man whose personal unity is weakened by the Fall. The fact that our primal parents saw fit to cover themselves with aprons of fig leaves means that they felt shame, but at the same time acted so as to avoid the utter disgrace of shamelessness. They were Fallen creatures, but not lost; the path to redemption through the Incarnation was still open to them. But shamelessness, the state which pornography encourages, is one in which people are truly lost. Pornography may not be able to effect its ultimate purpose—to bring about shamelessness. Conscience and personality are difficult to suppress completely. But the aim of pornography is to achieve the condition of shamelessness, and this is brought about by the gradual extinction of personality.

Fractionalization—Man Deprived of Unity

In the film, *Sleeper*, a man is awakened 200 years after he had been frozen, only to find himself an unwilling member of a totalitarian state. When this character, played by Woody Allen, overhears the medical team planning a lobotomy on his brain in order to make him adjust to life in totalitaria, he exclaims in terror: "No, that's my second favorite organ!" The joke is a common one and represents the fractionalization of modern man into a collection of unrelated organs.

We find the same fractionalization and reduction of man to impersonal, interchangeable parts in popular music. Prince, who earned more than $25 million in 1985, uses the following lyrics in his song "Let's Pretend We're Married":

Excuse me but I need a mouth like yours
To help me forget the girl that just walked out my door.

As pornography fractionalizes it isolates and alienates various human parts from each other. The result is a highly disunified man, a calamity that is very difficult to correct. The current telephone sex craze is a good illustration of this point. In 1982, when one particular pornography magazine set up the first x-rated "Phone Sex" operation (with sixty separate lines), a spokesman for New York Telephone confirmed that an average of 42,000 calls per hour were being placed.[38]

Pornography researcher David Alexander Scott cites the case of an FBI investigation into one porno service in New York City that was getting a staggering 500,000 calls per day.[39] The investigation uncovered the dismaying fact that in one day about one-third of these calls originated from the Pentagon. Steps were then taken to make it impossible for further calls of such a nature to originate from America's most populous bureaucracy, a virtual city that employs as many as 34,000 workers. The FBI was of the opinion that $10,000 a day for telephone porn is not a legitimate use of tax payers' money.

The Pentagon incident is a perfect illustration of how modern technology imposes a kind of Cartesian dualism which alienates mind from body. One does not need a particularly creative imagination to understand how office life in a federal bureaucracy can exemplify this dualism. The office worker labors within his small, confining cubicle. He has his computer, his desk, his typewriter, and his window overlooking the parking lot. His plastic rubber plant and the desk photo of his children are not enough to compensate for an atmosphere that may best be described as lifeless. Most of his daily contacts are with invisible subjects whom he reaches through mail, telephone, or intercom. His day is not rich and sensuous. It is deprived and uneventful, and he gradually begins to feel like a disembodied functionary. He looks forward to his coffee breaks, but even they have become tasteless. His body cries out for attention, like a pesky dog. He hungers for a brief moment of sensuous indulgence. He calls the sex telephone service and momentarily achieves some semblance of connection between mind and body.

Here, the inner disunity has progressed to so critical a stage that the office worker must call New York in order to re-establish contact between his mind and his body. The pornographic message presumably offers him a jolt, perhaps not unlike cardiac resuscitation, and he goes back to work again until the need arises for another electronic fix.

C.S. Lewis observed that something is radically deficient in the emotional life of modern man which creates the danger of cultivating "men without chests." He reminds us that "The head rules the belly through the chest."[40] This is to say that the mind rules the appetite through the emotions, a reflection of the Platonic notion that Reason in man must rule the mere appetites by means of the "spirited element." For Plato, Reason is the "forbidding principle," that reflects before it inhibits; Desire is the unreflecting appetite for pleasurable objects or for gratification of sense; and Spirit (*thymos*) is the assertive element, the propulsive faculty that is the agent or Reason, transmitting the verdict of Reason to the appetite and making that verdict effective.[41]

The chest—seat of emotions properly trained into stable sentiments—dispatches the liaison officers that are indispensable for uniting cerebral man with visceral man. It may even be said that without this middle element man is not man, for by his mind alone he is mere spirit, and by body alone he is mere animal. The chest preserves his unity by preventing him from disintegrating into a discarnate mind or an unreasoning brute, automaton or id. As Erich Fromm has written, "the naked ape with the computer brain would cease to be human, or rather, 'he' would not *be*."[42]

Psychotherapy offers its own corroboration of this view. We find this statement appearing in the literature: "today's patients, as a whole, seem to be preoccupied with the head and genitals in their dreams, and to leave out the heart."[43] Rollo May speaks of patients whose dreams are remarkably symbolic of our age. They include the brain and intellect, and the genitalia, but omit entirely the "seats of emotion, the thalamus, the heart and lungs, even the stomach. Direct route from head to penis—but what is lost is the heart."[44]   A graphic description of today's fractionalized, disunified man; and a condition consistent with the aim and purpose of pornography!

Because pornography bypasses the seats of emotion (even the stomach), it becomes easy to understand why it is unnourishing and addictive. People can never get enough of pornography because, like flattery, it feeds with an empty spoon.

Fictionalization—Man Deprived of Joy

There is no joy in things that do not exist. This explains why evil cannot bring joy since, in its essence, evil is nothing. In his *Screwtape Letters*, C.S. Lewis has his otherworldly-wise demon take pleasure in writing to his nephew, an apprentice in the business, about how, in the modern world, "we are more and more directing the desires of men to something which does not exist—making the role of the eye in sexuality more and more important and at the same time making its demands more and more impossible."[45]   Lewis expressed the same idea, though through a more conventional literary device, much earlier in his *Allegory of Love*, where he stated that lust seeks "for some purely sexual, hence purely imaginary, conjunction of an impossible maleness with an impossible femaleness."[46]

Pornography is fiction of the worst kind since it builds its enticements exclusively on lies and deceptions. It depends not on truth and realism, but on the tragic fact that lust disposes a man to believe anything.   Ulysses believed that nothing was more important to him than being with the voluptuous sirens that were, in fact, luring him to his death.   He cursed his crewmen and ordered them to release him so that he could fulfill his desires, but the crewmen, who were blindfolded and whose ears were filled with wax, paid no heed to his cries and rowed the boat to safety.

Pornography directs its victims toward dissolution and death. It peels away one aspect of reality after another until no reality remains. It bares all to reveal—nothing. The word "strip," in this context, is most appropriate. The pornographic film goes far beyond requiring the performers to disrobe. The process of stripping continues and affects the acting and the artistry, the dialogue and the drama, the plot and characterization; it effaces personality, erodes meaning, and eradicates love. The logical end-point of such pornographic stripping, as realized in "snuff" films, is death. Most assuredly, pornography is not in the interest of life.

Erich Fromm states that "intellectualization, quantification, abstractification, bureaucratization, and reification" are the very characteristics of modern industrial society. But these are not the very characteristics of modern industrial society. But these are not principles of life, but of mechanization. "People living in such a system," Fromm goes on to say, "become indifferent to life and even attracted to death."[47]

Canadian Business did a feature on the "Hard-core Capitalists" who find pornography a sufficiently lucrative venture to accept the legal and moral risks that come with the territory.[48] In the article there is an account of how illegal hard-core tapes are distributed. After calling a number in a classified ad, a person arranges a street-corner meeting to exchange cash for the tapes ($49.95 including $15 for courier charges). A typical example is *Bizarre Styles*, produced by a company that calls itself, significantly, Dead Parrot Productions. It contains whipping scenes that the pornography squad considers illegal. At the end of the tape, there are promotional trailers for other films that feature a variety of other sadomasochistic acts.

Because pornography feeds with an empty spoon, it cannot satisfy its consumers. Hence, the demand for advancing the stripping process, and the trade in illegal hard-core porn. But illegal porn is simply feeding with a larger empty spoon. The cloak and dagger scenario of the street-corner pickup is truly pathetic. Does the anxious consumer, who awaits the delivery of an illegal hard-core tape from an anonymous stranger, really believe that his clandestine purchase will provide him with something that is nourishing in any way? Does he believe that the morality squad exists to deprive people of glimpsing the deeper meanings of life that only uncensored pornography can reveal? Can he not begin to assess his situation in order to see himself as the sad victim of his own lust and of unscrupulous merchandisers? Might it not occur to him, as he awaits his illegal poison, that he is standing at the remotest edge of civilization and is bartering his self-respect for a taste of nothingness?

Pornography's last aim is to fictionalize the consumer, to make him unreal to himself, so that in the end nothingness meets nothingness and the result is nothing. In the moral void that pornography creates, it becomes impossible to understand how anything can be superior to anything else, how life can be better than death, civilization more desirable than anarchy, or creation preferable to destruction. D.H. Lawrence made this point most powerfully in his essay on "Pornography and Obscenity":

> The sex functions and the excrementory functions in the human body work so close together, yet they are, so to speak, utterly different in direction. Sex is a creative flow, the excrementory flow towards dissolution, de-creation, if we may use such a word. In the really healthy human being the distinction between the two is instant, our profoundest instincts are perhaps our instincts of opposition between the two flows. But in the degraded human being the deep instincts have gone dead, and then the two flows become identical. . . . It happens when the psyche deteriorates, and the controlling instincts collapse.[49]

Pornography seeks to fictionalize man and everything that surrounds him. It seeks a victory of formlessness over a world of form. It tries to reduce the created order of things to a level that is indistinguishable from waste and meaninglessness. Consequently, it makes joy impossible, because there can be no joy in an exchange of illusions and in the experience of nothingness.

Penthouse editor and publisher, Bob Guccione, appalled at the conclusions of the Meese Commission on Pornography, responded by taking his case before the American public. In one statement, which appeared throughout the country in various periodicals, he began by declaring that "The best thing about living in a free society is that we all have the right to pursue our own interests."[50] There are shades of Rousseauian idealism in this opening remark, and we are reminded of the opening sentence of Rousseau's *Social Contract*: "Man is born free; and everywhere he is in chains."[51] Guccione's opening gambit is equally unrealistic and abstract, very much like the pornography he publishes. But in a practical sense, not even he believes it. The closing words of his statement are forcefully presented in italics: *"Don't patronize a censor!"* The "censors" he has in mind and singles out for punitive action are store-owners who choose not to sell pornography. Apparently they do not have the right to pursue their own interests, which, from their point of view, are merely to operate retail stores that do not pander to prurient desires.

For Guccione, the "best thing" in our society is not really a thing at all, but an abstract ideology that absolutizes freedom while ignoring responsibility, and, despite its internal contradictions, somehow justifies pornographers dictating what retail merchants must sell. The society to which Guccione makes his allusions is a purely fictional one. It is an invention that results when thought refuses fact. The only way Guccione can defend his pornographic fiction is to set it within a larger "philosophical" fiction. This is why he and other publishers of pornography, like *Playboy's* Hugh Hefner, spend so much time developing their philosophy. What eludes them, however, is the realization that the true basis for philosophy's authority is the supremacy of fact over thought.[52] Philosophy, therefore, is anything but a fiction. It acknowledges the wide world of experience and humbly acknowledges what is. It does not indulge in ego-centric simplifications.

We expect a pornography publisher to defend his business interests, rather than be a disinterested social philosopher. At the same time, we should not be mistaken about what his allegedly philosophical declarations mean. They are not really philosophical; they are merely self-promotional. They do not address an incarnate world of persons who need to love each other in order that freedom and responsibility, life and morality, individuality and fellowship coalesce. They do not address that coherent structure in which men can live with each other in civic amity,[53] settle their differences in a spirit of justice, and experience their measure of joy. Rather, they address a fictionalized world in which virtue is unrealistic and pornography is harmless.

Through pornography we are fictionalized, fractionalized, depersonalized, privatized, victimized, and objectivized. By contrast, the Incarnation redeems us by restoring our reality and our identity, renewing our capacity for personhood and personal relationships, and reminding us of our intrinsic worth and our Divine sonship.

NOTES

[1]*Republic* III, 408e.

[2]*Ibid.*, 409d-e.

[3]I *Corinthians* 2:15.

[4]David A. Scott, *Pornography: Its Effects on the Family, Community & Culture* (Washington, DC: The Free Congress Foundation, 1985), p. 2.

[5]David Holbrook, ed., *The Case Against Pornography* (La Salle, IL: Library Press, 1972), p. 1.

[6]*Ibid.*, p. 2.

[7]*Ibid.*, "Sex in Bondage to the Modern Will: 'I'm Sorry Dear.'"

[8]Nikolai Berdyaev, *Slavery and Freedom* (New York: Scribner, 1944), p. 67.   "Materiality is objectivization, it is making existence into a thing." p. 96.

[9]Berdyaev, *The Destiny of Man* (New York: Harper & Row, 1960), p. 9.

[10]Holbrook, p. 7.

[11]Jon G. Murray, "Porn Shucked," *American Atheist*, June 1986, p. 5.

[12]*Ibid.*, p. 6.

[13]*Ibid.*, p. 5.

[14]*S.T.* I 98, 2.

[15]*Time*, "Tell All the Gang on 42nd St.," Oct. 19, 1970, p. 23.

[16]C.S. Lewis, *Mere Christianity* (London: Collins, 1961), p. 88.

[17]Scott, p. 11.

[18]Scott, pp. 24-5.

[19]Alfred S. Regnery, "The Effects of Child Pornography," *Policy Forum*, Vol. II, No. 15, Oct. 1985.

[20]Judith A. Reisman, "About My Study of 'Dirty Pictures'," *Washington Post National Weekly Edition*, July 1, 1985.   See also her article in *The Rutherford Institute*, Vol. 3, No. 1, Jan/Feb. 1986: "The Porno Industry: Giving Child Molestation its Stamp of Approval," pp. 10-11.

[21]James Check of York University, "Teens and porn: top consumers?" *Toronto Globe and Mail*, March 11, 1986, p. 1.

[22]Transcript of Proceedings: *U.S. Dept. of Justice, The Attorney General's Commission on Pornography*, Houston, Texas, Sept. 17, 1985.

[23]G.L. Simons, *Pornography Without Prejudice* (London: Abelard-Schuman).

[24]*Time*, Oct. 19, 1970.

[25]Jacques Maritain, *The Education of Man*, Donald & Idella Gallagher, eds., (Notre Dame, IN: University of Notre Dame Press, 1967), p. 183.

[26]Rollo May, *Love and Will* (New York: Norton, 1969), p. 57.

[27]Bardyaev, 1944, p. 31.

[28]Max Picard, *The Human Face* (New York: Farrar & Rinehart, 1930), pp. 3, 6, 7.

[29]May, p. 57.

[30]Edmund Rostand, *Cyrano de Bergerac*, tr. Brian Hooker (New York: Henry Holt & Co.), p. 143.

[31]Quoted in Marshall McLuhan, *The Mechanical Bride* (Boston: Beacon, 1967), p. 96.

[32]See Walter Berns, "Beyond the (Garbage) Pale or Democracy, Censorship & the Arts," *Censorship and Freedom of Expression*, Harry M. Clor, ed. (Chicago: Rand McNally, 1971).

[33]Pope John Paul II, *Blessed are the Pure of Heart* (Boston: Daughters of St. Paul, 1983), p. 76.

[34]*Ibid.*, p. 56.

[35]See Berdyaev, 1960, p. 236.

[36]Ernest van den Haag, "Is Pornography a Cause of Crime?" in Holbrook, p. 164: "Art may 'cancel lust' (as Santayana thought) or sublimate it. Pornography wants to desublimate it."

[37]Ian Robinson, "Pornography," in Holbrook, p. 169.

[38]"Sex Telephone Rings Off Hook," *Kitchener-Waterloo Record*, July 22, 1982.

[39]David A. Scott at the first convention of R.E.A.L. Women, in Toronto, Royal York Hotel, Feb. 2, 1985.

[40]C.S. Lewis, *The Abolition of Man* (New York: Macmillan, 1965), p. 34.

[41]Herschel Baker, "Platonic Humanism," *The Image of Man* (New York: Harper & Row, 1961), p. 46.

[42]Erich Fromm, *The Revolution of Hope* (New York: Harper & Row, 1968), p. 44.

[43]Leopold Caligor and Rollo May, *Dreams & Symbols* (New York: Basic Books, 1968), p. 108*n*.

[44]May, 1969, pp. 56-7.

[45]C.S. Lewis, *The Screwtape Letters* (New York: Time, 1963), pp. 69-70.

[46]C.S. Lewis, *The Allegory of Love* (New York: Oxford University Press, 1958), p. 196.

[47]Erich Fromm, *The Heart of Man* (New York: Harper & Row, 1968), p. 59.

[48]Liss Jeffrey, "Hard-Core Capitalists," *Canadian Business*, Nov. 1984, p. 44.

[49]D.H. Lawrence, *Phoenix*, p. 176.

[50]*American Atheist*, p. 4.

[51]Jean Jacques Rousseau, *The Social Contract*, tr. G.D.H. Cole (1762, New York: E.P. Dutton, 1947).

[52]Alfred North Whitehead, *The Function of Reason* (Boston: Beacon, 1958), p. 80.

[53]See M.J. Sobran, "Pornography," *The Human Life Review*, Vol. III, No. 3, Summer 1977, pp. 87-8.

7

Technologized Parenthood and the Incarnation

Natural pregnancy may become an anachronism. The two tiny laparoscopy scars, exposed by a bikini on the beach, will be as ordinary as our smallpox vaccination, but women will no longer have lost their figures in childbearing. The uterus will become appendixlike, though the ovaries will be as crucial as before. At the age of 20, each girl will be able to choose to be superovulated and her eggs collected and frozen, as it is known that babies conceived by young women are less likely to suffer from mongolism and other birth defects.[1]

"Technologized parenthood" is a disquieting expression. It represents the introduction of an essentially impersonal factor in an area that is replete with personal and transcendent meaning. Parenthood, which unites the natural with the supernatural, the present with the past and future, and spouses with each other and their progeny, is inevitably imperilled when it is allied with the one-dimensional processes of technologization. Techno-logized parenthood, then, is an attempt to fuse fundamentally discordant elements. And its inherent danger is in producing a split between technology and moral values, one that would result in the domination by technology of those moral values parenthood needs in order to realize its fulfillment in the distinctive forms of motherhood and fatherhood.

In his book *Mechanization Takes Command,* cultural historian Siegfried Giedion details how modern processes of mechanization have brought about a comparable split between thought and feeling. He found this split to be particularly evident in biology where it is commonplace to exclude feeling (especially those that carry moral implications) in order to bring everything under the reign of thought (for the purpose of rational control). By reducing the living organism to a mere assemblage of material parts, the entire dimension of feeling is thereby made irrelevant. According to Giedion, "in *biology* the animate being was considered simply as the sum of its separate parts assembled like those of a machine. Organic processes were regarded as purely physico-chemical in nature, as if an organism were a kind of chemical plant."[2]

Marshall McLuhan titled his first book *The Mechanical Bride* (1951) in order to jolt his readers into realizing that to the blind processes of mechanization and technologization nothing is sacred. Not even a bride, the quintessential image of unravished loveliness, would be spared. As a sequel to this work, McLuhan wrote *Culture is Our Business* (1970) to show how technology has created modern culture itself.

McLuhan's claims are amply validated by the contemporary verbal hybrids that are the logical offspring of our age of the "Mechanical Bride." Thus, we speak blandly of artificial flowers, astro-turf, synthetic food, and the bionic man. *The Love Machine, Heartbeeps, Electric Dreams,* and *The Computer Wore Tennis Shoes.* And we casually incorporate into our daily life such glaring incongruities as artificial intelligence, electronic voice-prints, atomic cocktails, and computer dating. We have been conditioned to take verbal incongruities in stride thereby preparing the way for the broad cultural acceptance of genetic engineering, test-tube babies, and technologized parenthood.

Surveying the threat that technology poses for life, McLuhan saw an antagonism between "technological determinism" and "organic autonomy,"[3] between the total dominance over life by technology and the freedom human organisms need in order to live and reproduce according to personal moral norms.

The invasion of technology into the domain of human sexuality began with contraception, which separates sex from procreation. Technologized parenthood is merely the converse of this separation. Whereas contraception means sex without babies, technologized parenthood means babies without sex (or at least without the fullness of the conjugal union).

Contraceptive sex violates the organic unity of sex and procreation. As a result, it leaves both these factors isolated and unprotected. Organically united, sex and procreation function together as protective complementaries. Procreation protects sex from degenerating into an act that makes pleasure primary; while bodified sex gives procreation a basis in personal intimacy, protecting it from exploitation by laboratory technicians and marketing managers.

The large scale cultural approbation of contraception has made technologized parenthood unavoidable, even though most people did not realize that when they accepted the separation of sex from procreation they were inaugurating the separation of procreation from sex.

When organic, incarnate unities are separated into isolated parts, a host of separations on moral, spiritual, and psychological levels take place concomitantly. One separation in particular is the focus of this discussion. It is the separation, through various modes of technological interventions in human reproduction, of parenthood from either motherhood or fatherhood. The fullness of both mother- and fatherhood demands the unification of procreation and bodified, conjugal love. As this unity is compromised or violated, the moral and spiritual meanings of mother- and fatherhood are proportionally jeopardized.

At the same time, the separation between parenthood and bodified mother- and fatherhood is occasioned by the split between thought and feeling. In this context, such a split is tantamount to separating the desire to control reproduction technologically from the willingness to recognize and protect the qualities that are peculiar to mother- and fatherhood. Parenthood in its most elementary form is achieved whenever there is the slenderest biological connection between progenitor and offspring. Parenthood is something humans share with all species of the animal and plant kingdoms. But mother- and fatherhood possess moral and spiritual dimensions that mere parenthood lack. It is precisely these dimensions that are at risk whenever there is an attempt to technologize parenthood.

We will examine five specific modes of technologized reproduction in order to illustrate the fundamental antagonism that exists between technologized parenthood and incarnate mother- and fatherhood. These modes are: 1) artificial insemination; 2) *in vitro* fertilization; 3) embryo transfer; 4) extracorporeal gestation; 5) surrogate motherhood.

Artificial Insemination

In 1884, a wealthy Philadelphia couple approached Dr. William Pancoast, a medical school professor. The couple had been trying to have a child, but without success. The doctor offered to help. Since the cause of the problem seemed to be with the husband, Pancoast looked for someone to donate semen to be injected into the wife's womb. He invited the best looking student in his class to be the artificial insemination donor (AID). The student complied and the doctor injected the semen into the woman which resulted in pregnancy.

Pancoast performed the artificial insemination while the woman was under anesthesia, and had not told her or her husband exactly what he had done. But he saw fit to change his mind once the baby was born. The infant bore such a striking resemblance to its biological father, that Pancoast felt obliged to explain to the husband what really transpired. The rich Philadelphian, happy to have a child, bore no grudge against the doctor. He asked only that his wife not be told how the child was conceived.[4]

We may ignore, in this instance, the factors of adultery, rape (involuntary intercourse), and gross deception. Our concerns here have to do with the effect of this technological procedure on the notion of fatherhood. While the Philadelphian was ignorant of the true paternity of the child, he believed that he was the father. After he was told that he was not the father, his wife continued to believe that he was. Thus fatherhood is made so tenuous as to be classified information that may or may not be revealed. At best, it is a mere belief. The husband believes he is not a father, the wife believes he is.

Dr. Pancoast's pioneer experiment in artificial insemination has prepared the way for no end of deception and confusion with regard to fatherhood. Technologized parenthood which allows a third party into the marriage relationship has proven to be extremely troublesome, even from the legal point of view. In Germany, for example, even a husband who consents to AID can disclaim his paternity anytime during the first two years of the child's life. In the United States, 15 states have laws which make a man who consents to the artificial insemination of his wife the legal father of the child. But in other states where no legal precedents exist, a husband who consents to AID and later changes his mind could conceivably charge his wife with adultery and refuse to support the AID child after a divorce.[5]

In order to avoid certain legal problems involving paternity, some doctors deliberately try to make the identity of the biological father impossible to determine. Dr. A.H. Ansari, an Atlanta, Georgia gynecologist, purposely inseminates a woman with a number of different sperm samples. He writes:

> Even in the same cycle, I may use four different donors for
> that individual. I do this so that if the case comes to court
> and they ask who the father is, it might give the lawyer a
> hard time to determine which of the four donors should be
> sued. As for the patient, she is just receiving biological
> material. She never meets the guy; she doesn't care whose
> semen you use.[6]

Not only does technologized parenthood through artificial insemination make fatherhood tenuous, it creates situations in which its specific determination is undesirable. Most medical students who provide semen for the customary fee of $50 probably do not desire to know whether or not their "biological material" has made them fathers. For them, such fatherhood places no moral or legal obligations whatsoever on them and is purely hypothetical. A sperm donor at the Tyler Medical Clinic in Los Angeles can contribute two or three times a week for $20 per "donation." Whether such a donor has sired tens or even hundreds of offspring is, as far as he is concerned, a mere abstraction.

A few legal cases in the United States show the extent to which the AID technology can erode the notion of fatherhood. In a New York State case, *Adoption of Anonymous*,[7] a woman's second husband petitions to adopt the child of his wife's first marriage. Her first husband refuses consent to the adoption procedure, claiming that he is the father. Confronted by this legal impediment, the petitioner argues that his consent is not needed since he is not the father, the child having been conceived by an anonymous donor. In this case, the judge ruled that the wife's first husband (though not the biological father) is the "parent" of the child and that his consent is required for the adoption of the child to another.

It is instructive, however, to note that not all courts have ruled or reasoned in the same way in similar cases. In California (*People v. Sorenson*, 1968), the Supreme Court reasoned that "a child conceived through AID does not have a 'natural' father;

that the anonymous donor is not the 'natural' father."[8] Another New York case (*Gursky v. Gursky*, 1963) went further in its depreciation of biological fatherhood:

> An AID child is not "begotten" by a father who is not the husband; the donor is anonymous; the wife does not have sexual intercourse or commit adultery with him; if there is any "begetting" it is by the doctor who in this specialty is often a woman.[9]

A child conceived through artificial insemination may have no natural father, may not be begotten by a father, or may be begotten by a "father" who is a woman! When fatherhood is reduced to the plane of the biological, it edges perilously close to oblivion. At the same time, the other dimensions of fatherhood—psychological, moral, spiritual, and legal—are subjects for the Court's sometimes arbitrary ruling.

Technologized fatherhood unravels the integrated totality of incarnate or unified fatherhood. The result is a separation of fatherhood from parenthood as well as a separation of the spiritual from the material, thereby greatly weakening fatherhood, making it appear nebulous, arbitrary, and even hypothetical.

In Vitro Fertilization

In artificial insemination, only the male gamete is isolated from the body. In IVF, both the male and female gametes are isolated from the body. Because these gametes can effect conception in a dish, totally apart from the bodified husband and wife, the impression is created that in a technical sense the gametes themselves are the parents.

This impression is not without its own biological analogues. Parenthood is conferred upon reproducing protozoans despite the fact that they are single-celled. Moreover, in ordinary mitosis, where somatic cells reproduce through replication, the resulting cells are called "daughter cells." Thus, parenthood is applied to biological entities of a single cell; why not to gametes as well?

The form of technologized parenthood we find with IVF creates the bizarre impression that a married couple's own gametes are challenging their claim to parenthood. This, of course, is reductionism in its extreme form. In a holistic perspective, it is the couple who become parents, not their gametes.

There is a time-honored axiom—*Actiones sunt suppositorum*—which means that actions belong to the person. We do not say that my eye sees or that my ear hears or that my feet walk. Rather, we say that I see with my eyes, I hear with my ears, and I walk with my feet. Since the source of our actions is in our subjectivity as persons, we attribute our actions to ourselves and not to one or another isolated part of ourselves. It is I who loves, not my heart; it is I who thinks, not my brain.

Likewise, it is the person who becomes a parent—in a specific way as a mother or father—and not the gametes. Technologized parenthood drives a wedge between specific parenthood which is predicated of the person, and technical or material parenthood which is predicated of the gametes or parts of the person.

By separating the gametes from husband and wife, and effecting new life in a Petri dish, *in vitro* fertilization fractures and fractionalizes incarnate parenthood, thereby allowing parenthood to be equivocally assigned to a variety of impersonal factors and to persons on a limited basis. The very expression "test-tube baby," although a journalistic creation, nonetheless suggests that the parent is a test-tube. And since the newly formed embryo can be implanted in a woman other than the one who contributed the egg, the gestational woman as well as the genetic woman are both called parents, though neither is a parent in the whole sense. Thus, *in vitro* fertilization creates the possibility of assigning parenthood to a variety of people in diverse ways and for different reasons.

On May 2, 1984, test-tube quadruplets were born in London to a Mrs. Janice Smale, who, according to her account, was married to Mr. Denis Smale. Upon investigation, however, it was learned that despite the name by which she identified herself, Mr. Smale is not her husband, but her boyfriend. "Mrs. Smale" is twice married and living apart from her second husband, pending divorce. Nonetheless, the doctors at Hammersmith Hospital in London fertilized six of her ova with Mr. Smale's sperm and implanted them in her uterus. Of the six embryos implanted, four survived.[10]

All the parties involved in the Smale case accept the moral premise that one need not be a husband before he becomes a father. They also endorse the premise that a wife may bear as many as six children at one time who are fathered by a man other than her own husband. The senior consultant of the hospital, who had been accused of actions "bordering on the unethical," defended his position by stating that it was certainly more ethical than that displayed at Bourn Hall where embryos were used merely as subjects for research.

By condoning such a procedure, the hospital is significantly weakening parenthood. Approving the separation of fatherhood from husbandhood (Mr. Smale) and husbandhood from fatherhood ("Mrs. Smale's" second husband) is not in the interest of integrated parenthood. Moreover, it lends support to the separation of parenthood from marriage, and procreation from love-making. Such a sequence of disconnections cannot but have a harmful effect on full mother- and fatherhood.

Technologized parenthood can easily by-pass a host of relevant moral concerns and bring about parenthood as a mere technological achievement. On the other hand, authentic parenthood, that is, full motherhood or fatherhood, is a personal realization that arises from a highly moral context of love, marriage, and conjugal intimacy. A truly progressive civilization must regard mother- and fatherhood as personal and moral realizations, and not as mere technological achievements.

Separating procreation from loving sexual intercourse depreciates love-making, but it also weakens parenthood and the bond that love forms between parent and child. This point may be expressed in a variety of ways, from the shock expressed by one reporter who exclaimed: "People are conceiving not in clinches, but in clinics!" to George Gilder's more reflective assessment of the matter: "By circumventing the act of love, *in vitro* conception takes another step toward dislodging sexual intercourse from its pinnacle as both the paramount act of love and the only act of procreation. It thus promotes the trend toward regarding sex as just another means of pleasure, and weakens the male connection to the psychologically potent realm of procreation."[11]

Embryo Transfer

Embryo transfer (also called "Artificial Embryonation") goes a step beyond what is logically implied by *in vitro* fertilization. With embryo transfer, an embryo (whether or not formed through IVF) that has already implanted in the uterus, is removed and transferred to the uterus of another woman. This technique is made available, fundamentally, for women who cannot conceive a child but are able to carry a child to term. A volunteer conceives the child (usually through artificial insemination) and then surrenders that child to the woman who will complete the period of gestation.

This technique effects the separation of pregnancy from motherhood and therefore assigns "motherhood" to various women on a limited basis. One woman supplies the egg, another the womb, yet a third might raise the child and supply the love and guidance. A child, therefore, may have three mothers: a genetic mother, a gestational mother, and an adoptive mother.

"We need to do a total rethinking of the notion of parenthood," writes Lori Andrews, a research attorney for the American Bar Foundation, and author of *New Conceptions*, a guide to the new reproductive techniques. "We don't even have a word," she adds, "that describes the relationship between a woman donating an embryo and a woman who is carrying the child."[12]

Two parents who are related to each other by virtue of a common relationship to a child are usually called husband and wife, and their relationship with each other is a spousal one. But the genetic mother is not the spouse of the gestational mother. These women may not even know each other. In our fragmented world of technologized parenthood, they may be regarded as partial parents, each contributing a part of what a traditional mother contributed by herself as a whole.

When the Harbor-UCLA Medical Center, the southern campus of the medical school of the University of California at Los Angeles, wanted to attract volunteers for its embryo transplant project, it placed the following ad in several community and college newspapers covering the South Bay area of Los Angeles:

> HELP AN INFERTILE WOMAN HAVE A BABY.
> Fertile women, age 20-35 willing to donate an egg. Similar to artificial insemination. No surgery required. Reasonable compensation.

Nearly 400 women responded to the ad, one of whom later became the genetic mother of the first child to come into the world as a result of the embryo transfer procedure. The staff at the Medical Center referred to their program as the Ovum Transfer Project.

The ad and the project are willfully deceptive. A volunteer was not asked merely to donate an egg or an ovum. She was asked to become pregnant in a manner that implied adultery, to undergo an early-stage abortion, and give her child up for adoption. In addition, she was asked to assume two rather serious risks in the event the lavage technique designed to remove her embryo failed. Either her child would be destroyed, or her pregnancy would persist. In the event the pregnancy persisted, she would be faced with either choosing a conventional abortion or carrying an unwanted pregnancy to term. She was also asked, by calling the child she conceived an "egg," to deny her own motherhood in this instance. It was convenient, from a merchandising point of view, for the Ovum Transfer Project to emphasize as much as possible the motherhood of their clients, who were to gestate the child, by denying the "partial" motherhood of the genetic mother.

By involving human reproduction with reproductive middlemen, and linking it more and more with principles of business and marketing, parenthood becomes increasingly arbitrary and may be assigned and re-assigned virtually at will. Parenthood ceases to be an aspect of one's identity as a human being, and becomes a title that one is able to purchase for a price. When the ad asks a fertile woman to donate an egg, it is trading on those altruistic sentiments that are evoked in human beings when they are asked to donate blood or to donate to the heart fund. But donating blood and donating one's own child are radically different from a moral standpoint. It is inhuman as well as unjust to treat a child as a donatable commodity. It is also unjust to mislead a woman into thinking that her embryo is only an egg.

One gestational mother in the Ovum Transfer Project expressed elation that, as she put it, "someone else's egg has grown in my body."[13] She expressed a desire to thank the genetic mother, but the latter does not know she is the donor. In 1982, Doctors Alan Trounson and Carl Wood of Melbourne's Monash University pioneered a method of freezing the surplus ova that their IVF patients did not need. In cases where an egg is frozen before it is thawed and fertilized, a woman may never know whether she is a mother. She is the female counterpart of the anonymous sperm donor. To her, her own motherhood is made hypothetical.

Closely associated with embryo transfer is a procedure known as embryo adoption. The technology is the same, but with embryo adoption donor semen is used instead of the semen of the recipient's husband. As the name suggests, with embryo adoption, a couple that has no genetic link to the embryo it adopts. Therefore, the child of embryo adoption has four parents: one who supplied the sperm, one who provided the egg, one who furnished the womb, and the male who raised the child as its father. What rights and status each of these parents have remains for the courts to decide. For example, do the parents who provided an adopted embryo's egg and sperm have visitation rights after that child is born? No doubt highly complex questions concerning intestate succession and will construction will have to be settled by the courts.

Extracorporeal Gestation

Extracorporeal gestation refers to the process by which the prenatal child is allowed to develop to term completely outside the mother's body in an artificial womb. No such womb has been developed to this point which could incubate a human being from conception to birth, but research continues. Scientists have predicted its arrival by the year 2000.[14] Bernard Nathanson contends that an artificial womb will be perfected much sooner. "A feasible artificial placenta is on the horizon," he writes, which he believes will lead to a reliable life-support system for the pregnancy outside its original host womb.[15] Nathanson also believes that such artificial uteri will be produced in sufficiently large quantities to solve the abortion controversy by providing incubation for all those unwanted fetuses who are deprived of a mother's womb.

Joseph Fletcher welcomes the artificial womb because it makes pregnancy more accessible to the scrutiny of watchful scientists:

> The womb is a dark and dangerous place, a hazardous environment. We should want our potential children to be where they can be watched and protected as much as possible.[16]

Isaac Asimov concurs, arguing that an embryo developing outside the body can be more easily monitored for birth defects and, eventually, for desirable gene patterns. But he also endorses extracorporeal gestation because it would help women gain an important measure of equality with men. If a woman could "extrude the fertilized ovum for development outside the body," he writes, "she would then be no more the victim of pregnancy that a man is."[17]

The Italian embryologist Daniele Petrucci claims to have developed an artificial uterus in which he kept a female human embryo alive for as long as 59 days. Progress is being made all over the world in developing an artificial womb, yet replicating the give-and-take equilibrium that exists between mother and child poses immense difficulties. Given such problems, the suggestion has been put forward to use nonhuman animals as surrogate mothers. Recently, cows have been suggested to serve as host "mothers." Emeritus professor of gynecology Ian Donald at Glasgow University states: "I can foresee the day when a human baby is born to a chimpanzee. That might happen within 20 years."[18] Edward and Steptoe, who delivered the world's first IVF baby have proposed that human embryos be implanted in such animals as sheep, rabbits, and pigs in order to study their early development.[19]

Current research on the subject of prenatal development indicates that the fetus is very much aware of his surrounding environment. For example, a newborn infant is able to distinguish his mother's voice from that of another woman, presumably from having heard it while being in the womb. Boris Brott, conductor of Ontario's Hamilton Philharmonic Orchestra, tells of an extraordinary musical experience he had which very well may be connected with his pre-natal life in the womb. While rehearsing a new musical score, Brott had a strong feeling of *déjà vu*. Though he had never seen or heard the piece before, somehow he already knew the cello part. Intrigued, he queried his mother, who is also a musician, and discovered that she had been rehearsing the same score while pregnant with him.[20]

Psychiatrist Tom Verny has reported in his book, *The Secret Life of the Unborn Child* (1981), that babies in the womb can experience a startling variety of sensations and emotions. To Verny, Boris Brott's story would not be at all surprising. But how deprived would a human fetus be if it developed in a metallic or bovine environment? One embryologist, Robert T. Francoeur, is most emphatic in his answer: artificial wombs, he says, "would produce nothing but psychological monsters."[21]

George Gilder fears that extracorporeal gestation on a large scale could ultimately make the womb obsolete.[22] If this came about, he reasons, women would lose their sexual appeal and cease to inspire men's love. By relegating procreation to science, the woman would forfeit her roles as wife as well as mother, and all the mystery and majesty that is inseparable from these roles. For similar reasons, Norman Mailer, in *The Prisoner of Sex*, closed his critique of radical feminism (which he regarded as essentially technocratic) by appealing to women not to "quit the womb."[23]

Extracorporeal gestation separates motherhood from parenthood most graphically, creating the impression that motherhood is something external to a woman's parenthood. But so basic a function of motherhood as gestation cannot be apportioned to a machine or a nonhuman animal without seriously violating the integrity of motherhood. From the eminently realistic viewpoint of a woman's incarnate identity, extracorporeal gestation does not represent liberation, but self-rejection.

Ethicist Paul Ramsey has criticized various modes of technologized parenthood for both depersonalizing and debiologizing human procreation.[24] These criticisms are perhaps nowhere more applicable than to extracorporeal gestation. To go a step further, extracorporeal gestation makes a woman's motherhood peculiarly discontinuous with her offspring to the point that she may inaugurate, abandon, and resume the motherly relationship with her child almost at will. She is initially a mother (genetically), but upon relegating the gestational phase of her motherhood to an artificial womb, she appears to discontinue her motherhood which she may later resume once the child is born.

Surrogate Motherhood

A surrogate mother is a woman who agrees to be inseminated with the sperm of a man whose own wife is not capable of either conceiving or carrying a child to term. She also agrees to relinquish any rights to the child and, once it is born, to deliver it into the custody of the sperm donor and his wife. For their services, surrogate mothers have received financial compensation that usually ranges from $5,000 to $30,000. Hence they are sometimes called "mercenary mothers."

The designation "surrogate mother" is misleading because it denotes that she is a substitute mother and therefore not the real or original mother. The surrogate mother is indeed the mother of the child, both genetically and gestationally. She is called a "surrogate" merely for psychological and commercial reasons in order to help the infertile woman, for whom the child is carried, feel that it is she who is the original mother. Such artful playing with language is a good indication of how easy it is to reapportion motherhood for reasons of convenience.

Legal experts are well aware of the fact that in the event a surrogate mother changes her mind and decides to keep her child, she would have that right. The strength of her position lies in the fact that she is the natural mother of the child, a point that is often obscured by misleading language.

A disproportionately high ratio of women who offer to carry babies for childless couples have had abortions. Dr. Philip Parker, a Michigan psychiatrist, found that of 125 women who took part in his study on surrogate motherhood, 26% had had abortions. Parker believes that many of these women want to have another baby and give it away as a way of compensating for the child they aborted.[25] On the other hand, applicants accepted for surrogate motherhood by Noel Kane, a Michigan lawyer who has popularized surrogate motherhood in the United States, all agree to have abortions if tests show the child they are carrying is deformed or mentally retarded.[26] Kane is the owner of the Infertility Center of New York, a profit-making agency which is involved in what one *Time* reporter describes as "the controversial business of matching surrogate mothers with infertile *parents*"[27] (emphasis added).

The association between surrogate motherhood and abortion also raises the question of whether a woman who is carrying a child for another woman can exercise her prerogative to abort the child if her own health is threatened, or even for personal reasons. Would a legal contract bind a surrogate mother to deliver the child she carries (apart from health considerations), whereas a marriage contract and a spousal relationship would be less binding? Should law regulate forms of technologized parenthood more rigorously than forms of natural mother- and fatherhood? Should a woman be less free to abort the child of another man who is paying her a large sum of money to deliver his child, than she is to abort her husband's child? On the other hand, can a lawyer for surrogate mothers *require* them to abort when there are problems with the pregnancy, whereas a woman's own husband cannot exact such a requirement?

The problems and issues that surrogate motherhood generates seems to be endless. We observe an instance of the confusion in reading the following ad for surrogates that appeared in a California newspaper and drew 160 responses: "Childless couple with infertile wife wants female donor for artificial insemination."[28]

A person might very well be led to believe that the advertiser is looking for a woman who will donate her egg for use in artificial insemination. The advertising couple was careful to avoid any reference to the word "mother," preferring to call a woman who conceives a child and carries it to term a "female donor."

In Oak Ridge, Tennessee, a woman who already had a 10-year-old son, served as a surrogate for her married sister who lived in New England. She presented her sister with a six-pound five-ounce baby girl.[29] In this case the baby girl was separated from her half-brother to be raised by her aunt, while regarding her own mother as an aunt. This confusion of identities and relationships is not uncommon among surrogate mothers. *Time* magazine did a personal profile on one surrogate mother who said of the child she conceived, carried, and delivered: "I feel like a loving aunt to her."[30] Technologized parenthood invariably causes women and men to take a detached view of their own motherhood and fatherhood. It makes it more difficult for them to act in accordance with who they are because they are confused about their own identities.

The desire to help an infertile couple to have a child is unassailable, even praiseworthy. But even the most laudable desires are not immune to the ill effects of sentimentality. The desire to help a couple to have a child does not justify adultery, kidnapping, or child-bartering. Sentimentality all too easily obscures reason, which must remain clear if we are to be assured that the means we choose are moral.

Robert Francoeur reports in his book, *Eve's New Rib*, an illuminating, as well as amusing, example of how a sentimental desire to help infertile couples can displace reason. At a convention of Catholic science teachers, a nun suggested that we might "update the charitable work of some religious communities and perhaps even establish a new order, a type of 'Sisters of Charity (or Mercy) for the Substitute Mother.'"[31] This enthusiastic and altruistic nun was proposing, in the name of Christian charity, that a religious order would come into being consisting of surrogate Sisters who would bear the children of infertile couples!

The most celebrated case involving surrogate motherhood is one that offers a more powerful argument against its practice than any philosophical argument could. Surrogate mother Judy Stiver of Lansing, Michigan gave birth to a child in January 1983 with a strep infection and microcephaly, a disorder indicating possible mental retardation. Alexander Malahoff, the man who had contracted for the child, decided that he did not want it and told the hospital to withhold treatment. Mrs. Stiver stated that she had not established a "maternal bond" with the child since she had not held him. According to Michigan legislator Richard Fitzpatrick, "For weeks the baby was tossed back and forth like a football—with no one having responsibility."

Then, with a macabre touch that Boston University health law professor George Annas said makes the soap operas appear pallid, Malahoff and Mr. Stiver had blood tests to establish the child's paternity and went on the "Phil Donahue Show" to await the results. During the show Donahue announced that Malahoff was not the father. The Stivers had intercourse shortly prior to the artificial insemination procedure; the child was genetically theirs.

Malahoff reacted by suing the Stivers for not producing the child he ordered and is attempting to recover the $30,000 he paid out in related expenses. The Stivers sued the doctor, lawyer, and psychiatrist of the surrogate program for not advising them about the timing of sex. Incredibly, the Stivers, who agreed to appear on the Donahue Show, took Malahoff to court for violating their privacy by making the whole affair public. And finally, the

Stivers claimed that their child's illness was caused by a virus transmitted by Malahoff's sperm.[32]

In a statement conveying uncommon moral insight, Roger Scruton helps us to understand how immeasurably weaker the bond between a surrogate mother and her child must become once society begins to disparage the significance of incarnation:

> Surrogate motherhood should be seen in its wider context—not as an answer to the problem of sterility but as the outcome of a revision in moral perceptions, comparable to that foretold in *Brave New World*. In surrogacy, the relation between mother and child ceases to issue from the body of the mother and is severed from the experience of incarnation. The bond between mother and child is demystified, made clear, intelligible, scientific—and also provisional, revocable and of no more than contractual force.[33]

As a direct result of denigrating the incarnational dimension of procreation, society begins to redefine parenthood in more legalistic and abstract terms. University of Texas law professor John Robertson, for example, states that current laws insufficiently protect what he calls "collaborative reproduction." His expression is ironic in that it implies neither motherhood, fatherhood, parenthood, marriage, or even procreation. At the same time, it describes in two well chosen words technologized parenthood's inevitable association with the mechanism of assembly-line production.

When we consider the various modes of technologized parenthood collectively, we discover that no feature of biological parenthood is considered indispensable for either mother- or fatherhood. With artificial insemination by donor (AID), a husband becomes a father despite the absence of his sperm, while his wife consents to conceiving a child by a man to whom she is not married; with artificial insemination by the husband (AIH), a man becomes a father apart from the conjugal embrace. With IVF, husband and wife become parents independently of sexual intercourse. In embryo transfer, a woman is considered a mother even though she is not the genetic mother. In extracorporeal gestation, a woman is called a mother even though she does not gestate the child. The surrogate mother foresakes nursing and rearing her child, and the mother to whom she delivers the child is neither the genetic nor gestational mother.

Collectively, these forms of technologized parenthood exclude virtually all those features that are naturally and traditionally associated with mother- and fatherhood: marriage, sexual intercourse, the genetic contributions of husband and wife, gestation, nursing, and child rearing. It should be amply apparent that technologized parenthood not only produces attenuated forms of mother- and fatherhood, but threatens their very meaning.

Combining different modes of technologized parenthood may make its threat to motherhood and fatherhood all the more salient. Lori Andrews speaks of "a busy career woman [who has] one of her eggs fertilized with her husband's sperm in a Petri dish and then implanted in another woman."[34] This same woman could arrange for her child to be reared by what some sociologists call "professional parents." And if this woman had her egg fertilized by a donor's sperm, she would have avoided marriage, intercourse, conception, pregnancy, gestation, lactation, nursing, and child-rearing, and still have retained the name *mother*. But in such a case, is the word "mother" anything more than an expression of will? Is this woman really a mother? Should not more be demanded of a mother than the donation of an egg?

To make matters even more confusing, some biotechnical revolutionaries would like to see men have children. Joseph Fletcher speaks enthusiastically about the prospect of a uterus being implanted in a human male's body and gestation achieved as a result of IVF and embryo transfer.[35] Fletcher also envisions hypogonadism being used to stimulate milk from the male's rudimentary breasts. The British magazine *New Society* claims that the technology to enable men to bear children is currently available and may eventually be utilized by homosexuals, transsexuals, or men whose wives are infertile.[36]

Paul Ramsey has good reason to argue, then, that "When the transmission of life has been debiologized, human parenthood as a created covenant of life is placed under massive assault and men and women will no longer be who they are."[37] By this, Ramsey means that human beings will not be able to live morally—that is, "be who they are"—if they do not understand that they are embodied persons, inviolable and incarnate unities of spirit and flesh. Neither a man nor a woman can "debiologize" themselves without denying and rejecting who they are as incarnate beings. Our modern scientific world has misled us into believing that matter is always something to be controlled, that thought is superior to flesh, that God's will is ever subject to technology's veto.

The various forms of technologized parenthood help people to have children, but they do not help them to become mothers and fathers in the full sense of these terms. Having a child does not make one a *father* or a *mother*; it only makes one a *parent*. Motherhood and fatherhood are fulfilling realizations of personal realities; they necessitate a continuity between incarnate being and moral act. In this regard, the notion of *fruitfulness* is more inclusive than that of *fertility*.

Husband and wife are fruitful through a loving intercourse in which they affirm each other's distinctive personal realities as man and woman in a way that creatively directs them toward the realization of their mother- and fatherhood. Fruitfulness, in contrast with fertility, is more than a mere exchange of gametes. One writer expresses this rich and elusive concept of fruitfulness between husband and wife in the following way:

> I not only affirm the unity of her person and nature as feminine but her integrity as an incarnate spirituality and its

dynamism, that is, her possible maternity through which I, in turn, find my paternity as a self.[38]

A boy becomes a man, a man becomes a husband, a husband becomes a father. Similarly, we speak of the development of the girl who becomes a woman, a wife, and finally a mother. These developments are by no means automatic; they require maturing processes, great personal effort, and the cooperation of other people and culture in general. Technology, however, always plans to make things happen automatically. Its intervention in the area of human procreation clashes with the slow and arduous processes that prepare the emergence of mother- and fatherhood. Nature always takes time. Technology is impatient. Nature is evolutionary. Technology wants to repeat the past. The clash, therefore, is between a rational plan and a natural process, between impersonal expediency and personal expression.

We do not help people to grow and fulfill their destinies by encouraging them to employ forms of technological parenthood which create the impression that there is no essential difference between fertility and fruitfulness, parenthood and mother- and fatherhood.

Technologized parenthood feeds on a philosophy of rational dualism that separates matter from morals and structure from activity. One does not behave as a mother or father simply because one is a parent in some legal or material way. It is not a legal document or a biological claim that makes one an authentic mother or father. Rather, the basis is in one's incarnate personhood and the willingness to embrace the moral responsibilities that mother- and fatherhood entail. There should be a continuity between matter and morals, form and destiny. Mother- and fatherhood should flow from their source in personhood as nature flows from the hand of the Creator.

When Gerard Manley Hopkins wrote, "He fathers-forth whose beauty is past change,"[39] he was drawing our attention to the fact that mother and father are verbs as well as nouns.

NOTES

[1]Edward Grossman, "The Obsolescent Mother: A Scenario," *Atlantic*, May 1971.

[2]Siegfried Giedion, *Mechanization Takes Command* (New York: W.W. Norton, 1969), p. 718.

[3]Wilbert E. Moore, ed., *Technology and Social Change* (Chicago: Quadrangle Books, 1972), p. 97.

[4]Lori B. Andrews, "Embryo Technology," *Parents*, May 1981, pp. 64-5. See also Robert Francoeur, *Utopian Motherhood* (London: Allen & Unwin, 1971), pp. 1-4.

[5]*Ibid.*, p. 65.

[6]*Ibid.*

[7]345 N.Y.S. 2d 430.

[8]*People v. Sorenson* in Mark Coppenger, *Bioethics: A Casebook* (Englewood Cliffs, NJ: Prentice-Hall, 1985), p. 5.

[9]*Ibid.*

[10]B.A. Santamaria, *Test Tube Babies?* (Melbourne: Australian Family Association, 1984).

[11]George Gilder, "The Bioengineering Womb," *The American Spectator*, May 1986, p. 22.

[12]Harris Brotman, "Human Embryo Transplants," *New York Times Magazine*, Jan. 8, 1984, p. 51. At a conference on "High-Tech Babymaking" in the Spring of 1986 sponsored by the Women's Research Institute of Hartford College for Women, keynote speaker Gena Corea expressed her concern that women could become merely collections of body parts, divorced from their procreative power and with a more tenuous self. At the same conference, Barbara Rothman expressed similar concerns about the process by which human reproduction is becoming "commodified." (*The Chronicle: Hartford College for Women*, Vol. 9, No. 1, Spring-Summer 1986.)

[13]*Ibid.*, p. 46.

[14]The prediction was made by the RAND Corporation/Douglas Aircraft studies. Cited in *Weekend Magazine*, Sept. 18, 1971.

[15]Bernard Nathanson, *Aborting America* (Garden City, NY: Doubleday, 1979), p. 282.

[16]Joseph Fletcher, *The Ethics of Genetic Control* (Garden City, NY: Doubleday, 1974), p. 103.

[17]Isaac Asimov, "On Designing a Woman," *Viva*, November 1973, p. 8.

[18]*St. Louis Post-Dispatch*, Sept. 9, 1984.

[19]*Kansas City Star*, Dec. 20, 1984.

[20]Pablo Fenjves, "When Does Life Begin?" *Woman's World*, Oct. 22, 1985.

[21]"Man Into Superman: The Promise and the Peril of the New Genetics," *Time*, April 19, 1971, p. 49.

[22]Gilder, p. 23.

[23]Norman Mailer, *The Prisoner of Sex* (New York: New American Library, 1971), p. 168.

[24]Paul Remsey, *Fabricated Man* (New Haven: Yale University Press, 1970), pp. 89 and 135.

[25]"Abortions Frequent among Candidates," *Toronto Globe and Mail*, Sept. 6, 1982.

[26]*Ibid.*

[27]Claudia Wallis, "A Surrogate's Story," *Time*, Sept. 10, 1984, p. 51.

[28]Elaine Markoutsas, "Women Who Have Babies for Other Women," *Good Housekeeping*, April 1981, p. 96.

[29]*Ibid.*

[30]Wallis, p. 51. See also *The Buffalo News*, Nov. 8, 1985 where Mrs. King, who carried a child for her sister, Carole Jalbert, said: "To this day, I feel like an aunt. I was just baby-sitting." See also *The Buffalo News*, June 26, 1986, "Woman Presents Sister with Gift of—Triplets," concerning what may be the world's first set of "surrogate triplets," presented as a "gift" to an infertile sister.

[31]Robert Francoeur, *Eve's New Rib* (New York: Harcourt Brace & Jovanich, 1972), p. 20. Fr. Owen Garrigan, author of *Man's Intervention in Nature*, asks whether a priest would violate his vow of celibacy if he donated semen to a sperm bank.

[32]The *Malahoff v. Stiver* lawsuit (No. 83-4734), was heard in federal district court in Detroit. Lori Andrews recounts the affair in the *American Bar Association Journal*. See also *Time*, Sept. 10, 1984, p. 53 and the Chicago (AP) wire service story in the *Kitchener-Waterloo Record*, Feb. 3, 1983, A10.

[33]Roger Scruton, "Ignore the body, lose your soul," *The Times* (London), Feb. 5, 1985, p. 10.

[34]Lori B. Andrews, p. 67.

[35]Fletcher, p. 45.

[36]London (AP), *Kitchener-Waterloo Record*, May 9, 1981, front page headline.

[37]Ramsey, p. 135.

[38]Terence P. Brinkman, S.T.D., "John Paul II's Theology of the Human Person and Technological Parenting," *Technological Powers and the Person*, ed. Rev. A. Moracwewski, O.P., *et al.* (St. Louis: The Pope John Center, 1983), p. 377.

[39]G.M. Hopkins, "Pied Beauty," *Gerard Manley Hopkins* (London: Unwin, 1953), p. 31.

8

Vocations, the Church, and the Incarnation

The current literature on the subject of religious vocations in the Catholic Church is not encouraging. Statistics alone provide a picture that is difficult to interpret as anything but bleak. Enrollment in American seminaries has declined from 48,992 in 1964 to 13,226 in 1980,[1] a reduction by 73 percent. During that time, approximately 200 seminaries were closed.[2] In addition, during the eight-year period between 1967 and 1975, some 30 percent of American priests left the active ministry.[3] And forecasters predict that by the year 2000, there will be only half as many priests in the United States as there were in 1975.[4] The broad statistical picture with respect to nuns is equally disturbing, showing that between 1967 and 1978, the Church in the United States lost more than 40,000 Sisters.[5]

The current vocation situation has been repeatedly described as a crisis. Now we all know that this word is immensely overworked, often used to heighten interest in whatever is being discussed. Nonetheless, its application to the current vocation situation is fitting. At the same time, however, we should understand that the word "crisis" does not necessarily express pessimism. A crisis is a moment when all the relevant forces that bear on a situation come together in such a way that the next stage in the development of that situation is not irrevocably determined. A crisis is a crossroad that represents alternatives of opposite value. In Chinese ideograms this meaning is conveyed with force and clarity, for here the word "crisis" is expressed in two characters, of which one stands for danger, the other for opportunity. We shall regard the "vocation crisis" as a time that is rich with opportunities for good things, but, in order to offset its attendant danger, a time that demands immediate attention, enthusiasm, intelligence, and great love.

Recent literature on the vocation crisis points consistently to a single dominant cause, namely, the lack of encouragement a potential candidate to the religious life receives from family members as well as religious. Sociologist William McCready, of the National Opinion Research Center at the University of Chicago, has done a study on attitudes toward religious vocations. On the basis of his study, he draws the following conclusion:

> If the Church wants young people to think about and to follow priestly and religious vocations, then priests, religious, and immediate families must increase their encouragement of the young people in this regard.[6]

McCready also points out that, overall, the importance of the lack of encouragement is much greater than the celibacy issue, because the former deprives people of the opportunity even to think about pursuing a religious vocation.[7] Other sociologists agree with McCready's findings, noting what they refer to as "a considerable decline in enthusiasm for recruiting."[8] This same conclusion has been reached by studies on the diocesan level.

The Vocations Office staff and the Vocations Advisory Board of the diocese of Camden, New Jersey, for example, found that "lack of encouragement on the part of both parents and Religious" is the number one cause of declining enrollment in their diocesan seminaries.[9] The investigators in this study generally agree that today's parents are less inclined to view the religious life as a vocation option comparable to professions such as law or medicine. And they cite other surveys that confirm their observation: for example, one survey conducted in the late 1960s disclosed that 80 percent of Irish-American parents were supportive of a child who expressed a desire for a religious vocation; a similar study in 1974 showed that only 43 percent of such parents were supportive.[10]

Father Kenneth Baker, S.J. made the following statement on the editorial page of *Homiletic and Pastoral Review* back in July of 1973:

> During the past year I have quizzed priests from all parts of the country on whether or not they encourage young men to enter the seminary. To my amazement I have discovered that most do not. The two principle reasons given for this conduct are: 1) the breakdown of discipline and morals in the seminary, and 2) the absence of solid Catholic teaching.

In the ensuing decade, Fr. Baker encountered many more priests who do not and will not encourage vocations. The reason cited for this lack of encouragement is that they have seen too many young men, whom they had encouraged, go to the seminary and lose their faith. Reviewing what he had written earlier, Fr. Baker declared in a 1982 editorial that "Today I have no reason to change that view. I am convinced that it was correct then and that it is still correct."[11]

We find, in the following declaration by one priest, the kind of attitude Fr. Baker has encountered: "Most of us would be very slow to encourage a really pious young person to be a priest or sister today. We wouldn't want to be responsible for the losing of their faith."[12]

On a superficial level, the mere lack of encouragement is an occasion for optimism for some people. William McCready, for example, remarks that "If we begin to upgrade the encouragement that young people receive from religious professionals and from their families with regard to considering a religious vocation, we might easily have twice as many vocations in the near future as we currently have."[13]

Nonetheless, the lack of encouragement phenomenon is not the result of mere inadvertence. The vocation problem has deep roots which remain essentially unaffected by a change of strategy or a mere external face-lift. There are substantial reasons that account for the lack of encouraging vocations and these reasons must be exposed before the situation can be reversed.

Another inappropriate response to the vocation crisis is to regard the shortage of vocations as something good, even conferred by God. This stance suggests that there is nothing we need to do but sit back and enjoy the unfolding of God's will. A Catholic writer, who is a popular syndicated columnist, advises that "The Holy Spirit has given us the reality of fewer vocations to the ordained priesthood, perhaps to inspire the fulfillment of the potential of the priesthood of the laity."[14]

The existence of fewer priests may be a challenge to a profundity of prayer and action, but of itself cannot be construed as an inspiration. In certain areas where religious vocations are thriving—Poland, for example, or any number of particular parishes in North America—it would be irreligious to think that here the action of the Holy Spirit is being thwarted. The apostolate of the laity is meant to complement that of the clergy, not compete with it, much less replace it. The priest has an irreplaceable function in the Church in making God present to man through the sacraments. Accordingly, Vatican II teaches that "No Christian community . . . can be built up unless it has its heart and center in the celebration of the most Holy Eucharist."[15] It would be more logical to view a plenitude of vocations as a sign of the spiritual health and vitality of a Christian community. At any rate, Pope John Paul II has stated that "Numerous vocations are a sign of the generosity and maturity of a Christian community."[16] And it also reflects the mind of the bishops present at the 1980 Synod on the Family who stated that one of the fruits of an effective family ministry "ought to be the flourishing of priestly and religious vocations."

In linking vocations to the moral and spiritual health of the Christian community, the Holy Father is drawing attention to the fact that causes exist on different levels, for generous and mature Christians surely will not fail to encourage vocations. Let us use a prosaic model to illustrate the point. A baseball team loses because it does not score enough runs. But it does not score enough runs because its hitting is weak or because its pitching and defense give up too many runs. These causes, in turn, have their own underlying causes which may involve poor player attitudes, poor coaching, or even lack of support from the fans. Causes have causes. There is a crisis in vocations because of a lack of encouragement. But this lack is connected to another set of underlying causes: a lack of confidence in seminary formation, for instance. This cause, in turn, is related to a deeper cause, and so on. The first step in dealing effectively with the vocation crisis, then, is to lay bare the cause which is at the very root of the problem. And if we discover this cause, will it not be that institution which is the fundamental institution of both the Church and society, namely, the family?

In his apostolic exhortation on the *Community of the Family* (*Familiaris Consortio*), the Pope states:

> Indeed, the family that is open to transcendent values, that serves its brothers and sisters with joy, that fulfills its duties with generous fidelity, and is aware of its daily sharing in the mystery of the glorious Cross of Christ, becomes the primary and most excellent seedbed of vocations to a life of consecration to the kingdom of God.[17]

The Holy Father reiterated this statement in December of 1982 while delivering a homily to a gathering of parents and seminarians. On this occasion he added these pertinent words:

> Normally a vocation is born and matures in a healthy, responsible and Christian family background. It becomes

> rooted precisely there and draws from it the possibility of
> growing and becoming a strong tree, laden with ripe fruit. . .
> The seminary exercises . . . a unique and determinant role.
> But everything starts from the family and in the last instance
> everything is conditioned by it.[18]

Because the family is the primary "seedbed" of religious
vocations, and an indispensable factor in bringing vocations to
their maturity, it follows that a crisis in the family would
inevitably precipitate a crisis in vocations. But is the family in
crisis? To this question today's observers of the family situation
respond with virtual unanimity. Today's family is indeed in crisis,
and this is particularly true of the family in America. A falling
birthrate and a rising divorce rate, the widespread practice of
contraception, sterilization, and abortion, a greater tolerance of
adultery and pre-marital sex, a confusion of the roles of the sexes,
and an erosion of parental authority are some of the pertinent
factors that attest to the family's critical condition. Novelist John
Updike captures the sense of extreme confusion that
characterizes our time when he speaks of married couples who
exist in "one of those dark ages that visits mankind between
millenia, between the death and rebirth of gods, when there is
nothing to steer by but sex and stoicism and the stars."[19] Updike's
allusion to an attitude of fatalism is of special interest in the
context of vocations, for only Christians believe in vocations, in
actively responding to God's personal calling to serve Him in a
particular way of life; pagans do not believe in vocations, they
passively drift into whatever state of life fate has decreed for
them.

Reverend Michael Windolph, O.F.M., who has been
involved in parish work for more than thirty years, has come to
believe that the "vocation crisis in the married state" has
intensified in recent years to the point where it has "become a
major factor in the basic vocation crisis of the Church."[20] Fr.
Windolph's words carry a special authority on this subject since 9

of his parents' 12 children became religious: five nuns and four priests.

Perhaps the single most persuasive indication of the unhappy condition of today's American Catholic family is the alarming frequency with which husband and wife dissolve their marriage. According to Church figures, in 1981 there were an estimated 77 annulments granted to American Catholics for every one in 1968, constituting 70 percent of all annulments granted by the Catholic Church throughout the world.[21] More than twice as many annulments are granted to American Catholics than to the rest of the world's Catholic population combined. Over a 15 month period of adjudication by the Brooklyn diocesan marriage tribunal, 768 annulments were granted out of a total of 768 requested.[22] There are now more than eight million divorced Catholics in the United States.[23] Some observers have interpreted such figures as being a strong indication that the Catholic Church in the United States has "already seceded from Rome on this matter so central to Catholic moral teaching and sacramental life."[24]

Divorce produces consequences that are severely detrimental to the kind of family atmosphere that is needed to nourish vocations. The rate of mental illness among divorced men is over five times as high as that for married men and for divorced women it is almost three times as high as that of their married counterparts.[25] In addition, as sociologists point out, divorce is "damaging to children—not only when they are young but also later in their adult life—and that this, in turn, hurts society, which must cope with the damaged children's anti-social behavior or impaired ability to achieve."[26] Since 1972 over one million children under the age of eighteen have been affected by divorce in the United States, and about 52 percent of them live in single-parent families with an income below the poverty level.[27] As research has shown, most people who follow a religious vocation come from a happy and contented home-life.[28] Divorce, with its train of disruptive and demoralizing sequelae, must be regarded as having a profoundly negative influence on the nurturing of vocations.

Stability and spiritual wholeness must be established in the family if it is to be what it should be in providing children with the proper context in which religious vocations will be received and nourished. In such a context, certain fundamental verities are imparted without which a religious vocation is unlikely to take root and develop. In this regard, the family is indispensable, for these verities—Christian in their essence—are either ignored or staunchly opposed by the world. We will consider four of these verities and indicate briefly how they correlate with a religious vocation.

Each State of Life is a Vocation

Perhaps the most significant factor in the instability of Catholic marriage today is the failure on the part of husband and wife to understand and accept their marriage as a vocation. Like many of their non-Catholic counterparts, they approach marriage with a high degree of self-interest in mind, a fact that is only slightly obscured by the use of more respectable psychological terms such as "self-fulfillment" and "self-realization." This point is made even more clear by the popular clichés that are offered to rationalize divorce or separation: "we were not growing together," "it just wasn't working out," or "I didn't feel fulfilled." In these cases, marriage is viewed more as an opportunity for individual and mutual satisfactions than as a generous response to a divine call and an opportunity to fulfill God's Will in a particular state of life. American Catholics have high expectations when they marry, but these expectations are often centered on fulfilling individual needs rather than on being prepared to make the kind of sacrifices required by a marriage that has a vocational and sacramental dimension.

Individual satisfactions are important, even necessary, but they should be a consequence of a good marriage, not a motive for being married. It is axiomatic that happiness recedes in direct proportion to the effort we spend in pursuing it. Happiness, as its etymology indicates, is something that happens. First, we must seek the kingdom of God. There are more professionals and support groups available today for assisting troubled marriages than ever before in history, but they are of little help if they place the individual satisfactions of the couple first.

Nonetheless, it would seem that even a stable and happy household is an inappropriate setting in which to engender a vocation to the religious life. The ancient maxim, "like begets like," suggests that a happy marriage should inspire children to emulate what made their parents happy, surely not to renounce marriage and sexual expression along with it. But the couple that is married in the Lord, and regards its marriage as a vocation, teaches its children that happiness derives from how well one fulfills God's calling and not how adroitly two people fulfill each other. In a "vocational" marriage, children will receive the message that their parents are happy not because marriage makes people happy, but because they have been true to their calling. At the same time, a "vocational" marriage is the logical environment in which other "vocational" marriages will be first awakened.

Reverend Basil Pennington, O.C.S.O., who is a "Vocation Father" at St. Joseph's Abbey in Spencer, Massachusetts, writes:

> One of the factors that undermines the vocation to Christian marriage today is that there are so few unions within which the sacramental dimension is fully alive and manifest, to call forth a recognition of this same grace and vocation of Christian marriage in their own children and others.[29]

Husband and wife who live their marriage as a vocation will inevitably assume the role of vocation directors and, cooperating with God's grace, awaken and guide their children to whatever state of life God is calling them to fulfill.

Truth is Paradox

Christianity is a religion built around paradoxes. The Annunciation announces that a virgin will be a mother. The Incarnation signifies that God has become man. The Nativity proclaims that an infant is king. The Resurrection means that in death there is life. In order to embrace a Christian life one must be profoundly acquainted with the fact that all life's basic truths are grasped in the form of paradox. Family life provides a unique opportunity for acquiring the wisdom that is inherent in paradoxes. The proper relationship between husband and wife is paradoxical inasmuch as each partner must blend complementary opposites—mind and heart, strength and tenderness, vision and practicality—into a single, unified experience of parental care. Parents use their *authority* to promote the *liberty* of their children. And children have a greater controlling influence on their parents' lives in proportion to their own weakness—the infant rules the household.

Such paradoxes, which inevitably require some degree of tension and struggle, stand in striking contrast with the secular tendency to dissolve all difficulty and seek but one simple goal, to live, as T.S. Eliot has described it, in "uncomplicated adjustment to an uncomplicated world." Secular society, with its abiding faith in the two-income family and the two-car family, in permissiveness, in privacy, in unisex, in reproductive freedom, in day-care centers, and in no-fault divorce, tries to make family life easier, but in so doing, makes it virtually impossible. As one sociological observer points out:

> [Today's family] is no longer seen as a compensatory institution, but as a community whose end is the support, the fulfillment, and the health and satisfaction of its

individual members. The family no longer serves mainly to nurture the citizen, the religious person, or even the economic person. It is there to serve "psychological man"....[30]

In contrast, the conciliar decree "Perfectae Caritatis" states that "Parents should develop and protect religious vocations in the hearts of their children by training them to behave like Christians."[31]

A good Christian family is constantly at work forging character in the rigors of life's perennial paradoxes, reconciling husband with wife, child with parent, brother with sister, individuality with community, man with God, and a natural existence with a supernatural destiny. And it is precisely this kind of family life that provides the right kind of preparation for the religious life.

One religious, writing in *Sisters Today*, underscores the essential importance in the lives of all religious of reconciling opposites. She writes:

> The religious life in which I persevere is not one of happy, fixed finality. It is rather one that is open to the clash and tensions of opposites. Here chastity meets human sensuality, obedience counters responsibility, and poverty faces the needs of personal and community security.[32]

Perhaps the most relevant paradox for today's religious involves reconciling the temporal with the timeless, particularly in the context of appropriate renewal. This very expression, "appropriate renewal," is the original translation of Pope Paul VI's words "De Accommodata Renovatione" as they appear in the title of his "Decree on Appropriate Renewal of the Religious Life" in *The Documents of Vatican II*. "Appropriate" seems to be the proper translation of the Latin word *accommodata*, which is ordinarily translated as "suitable to," or "adapted." "De Accommodata Renovatione" has also been translated as "on the adaptation and renewal." However, in the Flannery edition of

The Documents of Vatican II, a new and somewhat problematic translation of these words appears: "The Up-To-Date Renewal." The use of the catch phrase "up-to-date" may obscure the essential message of the decree which urges the reconciling of the present with the past, the contemporary with the original. Nonetheless, the text of the decree is quite clear:

> The appropriate renewal of religious life involves two simultaneous processes: (1) a continuous return to the sources of all Christian life and to the original inspiration behind a given community and (2) an adjustment of the community to the changed conditions of the times.[33]

Paradoxically, everything that is original goes back to the origin; everything that renews, repeats the old. If a community is simply "up-to-date," it invariably identifies itself too closely with the world and loses sight of its obligation to fuse the temporal with the timeless. In opposition to the simplistic and non-paradoxical pre-occupation with bringing everything "up-to-date," C.S. Lewis has remarked that "everything that is not eternal is eternally out of date."

Catholic historian James Hitchcock points out that "religious communities that combine renewal with fidelity to the spirit of their founders have, based on statistical projections, very bright futures." On the other hand, those communities that try to renew themselves on the basis of present trends, "are doomed to near extinction by the end of this century."[34]

Sister Bernadette Counihan, O.S.F. has analyzed community renewal approaches under three categories: the *static* approach that is resistant to change; the *revolutionary* approach that breaks with the past; and the *evolutionary* approach which combines change with continuity. She finds that only the latter approach, which accepts the tension that comes with trying to balance opposites, embodies the true spirit of Vatican II.[35] Many others have made the same discovery and, in addition, have alluded to the practical benefits associated with this latter approach. Fr. Thomas Dubay, S.M., for example, writes:

> Travel and contacts throughout the country indicate that congregations that have opted either for an immobile rigidity or for a secular life style have lost often more than 25 percent of their membership, while those that have renewed according to the whole mind of Vatican II have usually lost far less. The first types attract few, the second often many. These are facts, not opinions.[36]

Equally important to emphasize, however, is the fact that while balancing the best of the new with the best of the old represents a paradoxical polarity (or tension) that is strengthening, both for the individual and the community, the attempt to live any mixture of the static, revolutionary, and evolutionary approaches within the same community represents a contradictory polarity (or tension) that is divisive. Paradoxes are possible, but contradictions are impossible.[37] There are enough legitimate challenges for the religious, and these are clearly spelled out in the Vatican II Documents, but to challenge the challenge can only be disruptive and counterproductive. Nonetheless, there are times in everyone's life when the authentic challenges seem awesome while the impossible challenges seem attractive. Yet authentic challenges are precisely what are needed to awaken us to life and to give our capacities a creative purpose; evading these challenges can lead only in the opposite direction.

The Family—School of Faith

It is by no means an insignificant fact that while religious communities are hoping to increase their numbers, the typical Catholic family in North America is anxious to limit or reduce its own. In terms of simple arithmetic, such a situation is bound to have an adverse effect on the total number of people called to pursue the religious life. Research has shown that relatively few candidates for religious life come from families in which they were the only child.[38] At the same time, sociologists predict that as many as forty percent of women born in the 1950s will remain childless or have only one child during their lifetimes.[39] Naturally, an only child will not receive much parental encouragement to enter a religious life. A great burden is placed on him to fulfill other parental expectations. He is the only heir to carry on the family business, or to inherit the family fortune; or the only child who can carry on the family name, or give his parents grandchildren. Given this reality, it may be more appropriate, in praying for vocations, first to pray for progeny!

At the same time, economic pressures and materialistic inducements have considerably altered society's attitude toward having children. People commonly view children today as economic liabilities, as restricting the mobility of a family "on the go," as contributors to pollution and the "population crisis." In order to keep pace with the rising expectations of an affluent society, the modern couple carefully *plans* its family, fully cognizant of the negative impact unplanned children can produce. In many instances, the *plan*, with its technological arsenal of contraception, sterilization, and abortion, replaces *faith*.

According to American bishops, statistics show that almost 80 percent of all Catholic women in the United States use contraceptives.[40] This is an exceptionally high figure, perhaps unrealistically so, since it does not include cases where the woman is sterile, either by chance or by choice. Nor does it include cases where the man is the sole contraceptor. In addition, according to a recent Gallup poll, 44 percent of Catholics surveyed believe that their Church should relax its standards forbidding abortion in all circumstances.[41] Such faith in technological modes of family planning that run counter to Church teaching often go unopposed by the clergy. One study indicates that only 29 percent of priests in the United States believe that contraception is "intrinsically immoral."[42] And a number of celebrated cases have been popularized by the press in which religious have worked very hard so that women could have easier access to abortion.

It is difficult to resist the thesis that many religious vocations are contracepted or aborted as a result of a plan of technological control usurping the more Christian attitude of faith in God's Providence. A fearful and ungenerous family environment can hardly be expected to foster vocations for the religious life since that life is essentially a life of faith. Husband and wife are united to God through their conjugal intimacy. Contraception violates this intimacy. The religious is united to God in his own special way through his vows. A contraceptive attitude carried over into the religious life would do violence to this union.

One religious, in criticizing the lack of faith prevalent in marriage today, has made this observation:

> For many, a Church wedding means only that: a wedding in a church. If they have trouble keeping faith with each other is it surprising that they should have no faith or trust in God in accepting and living up to the serious responsibilities of the married state? Their faith and trust have been put in the pill and the psychiatrist.[43]

Only faith can understand marriage. Only faith can tell us of the unbreakable bond that exists between God and His people as revealed in Jesus Christ. Faith is necessary to be open to the transmission of life, just as it is necessary to be open to the transmission of a religious calling.

The Mission of the Family

The distinction is made between a *ministry* and a *mission*. A ministry provides what is lacking in people's lives. It focuses on meeting their specific material, physical, psychological, and spiritual needs. Health professionals minister to people's needs, as do clergymen and parents. A mission, on the other hand, goes beyond a ministry. It flows directly from a life of intimacy with God in a community of faith. When a hospital patient recovers his health, he is discharged. The hospital extends no mission to him apart from its ministry. But a family, as Pope John Paul II has explained in *Familiaris Consortio*, "has *the mission to guard, reveal and communicate love*, and this is a living reflection of and a real sharing in God's love for humanity and the love of Christ the Lord for the Church his bride."[44]

It is the mission of the family to make, through the unique love it has for its own members, disciples for the Church who will bring God's Word to all nations of the world. The family, then, is the novitiate for all missions in the Church. According to one religious writer:

> The primary mission of the family is to reveal the Church to itself. This is not accomplished by providing services to the Church as a family: that would be family ministry. Rather, it comes about by living out in the midst of the Church the meaning of family, not just as model but also as a leaven, to call the people of the Church to live as the family of God.[45]

The contemporary family has forgotten its mission or has collapsed it into a ministry. The result has been an almost exclusive preoccupation with producing "fulfilled individuals." Individualism is a central value in American society and has had a powerful influence on Catholics. Consequently, they commonly view family, religion, and work as projects for the expression of self rather than as activities that have transcendent implications that involve cooperative and creative relationships with others. Sociologists of religion have noticed a pronounced tendency in recent years for people to interpret religious faith and practice in psychological terms. In many cases, the counselling office has replaced the confessional. In seminaries, there is the widespread problem of promoting a faith that an individual teacher has, but not the faith of the Church. Where the family conceives itself as having no mission beyond its ministry, it comes to be regarded as just one of many types of structures that minister to individual needs. Professional groups displace rather than complement the family when they claim to offer the individual better service. But the family that understands and fulfills its mission will prepare children to understand the mission of Christ and the mission of His Church. *Lumen Gentium*, Vatican II's most important dogmatic document concerning the nature of the Church, begins by emphasizing the central importance of the Church's "mission" of "bringing men to full union with Christ, since mankind today is joined together more closely than ever before by social, technical, and cultural bonds."[46]

The fundamental affinity between the family and the Church is made evident by language. Priests have the common title of Father, while the religious Brothers and Sisters are addressed by these familial titles. The head of a female order is a Reverend Mother. The head of a monastery is called the "abbot," which is derived from the Aramaic word "abba," meaning "father." Vocational directors often identify their work as "spiritual parenting." And the Pope is called the Holy Father.

In recent years, the Church has strongly and repeatedly emphasized this affinity between family and Church. Vatican II speaks of the family as a "domestic Church." "The family," it states, is "the domestic Church. In it parents should, by their word and example, be the first preachers of the faith to their children. They should encourage them in the vocation which is proper to each of them, fostering with special care any religious vocation."[47] During the 1980 Roman Synod on the family, this expression "domestic Church," borrowed from the Second Vatican Council, was perhaps the most common designation of the family.[48] The synod also emphasized that marriage is a vocation that has many similarities to a priestly or religious vocation. In his apostolic letter, *Familiaris Consortio*, the Holy Father states that, "The Christian family constitutes a specific revelation and realization of ecclesial communion, and for this reason too it can be and should be called "the domestic Church."[49]

The Church as a whole, like the living human body, has an organic character. All the members of the Church are united together in such a way as to help one another. When one member suffers, all the other members share his pain, and the healthy members come to minister to his needs. Members of the Church do not live for themselves alone, but also to help their fellow members. Unlike the body, however, each member of the Church has his own individual subsistence and is able to enjoy his own personality. This particular kind of organic character of the Church, in which Christ penetrates every part and is the source of every grace, is called the Mystical Body.[50]

With the Mystical Body explicitly in mind, Vatican II urges all members of the Church to be faithful to their vocations and the vital and unique roles they are called to play. In making this plea it quotes St. Paul's remark that "all members have not the same function" (Romans 12:14).[51]

Too much stress on individual freedom dismembers the Church. We feel the pervasive shattering effect that sends shock waves throughout the Mystical Body when members seek to be what they are not and to do what they are not called to do. A Church is not whole or healthy when nuns want to be priests, priests want to be married, married people want to be divorced, divorced people want to remarry, re-divorced people want to live together, and ex-cohabitants want compensation. A society or a Church or a religious community begins to decay when it releases each individual to the freedom of his own impotence.

The Church is organic, and each person is called to play a special role, one that demands an exacting reconciliation of individual talents with membership in the Mystical Body. One vocation helps to fulfill another, as God's saving Word resounds from parent to child, family to family, Christian to Christian, throughout a varied but cohesive Church. Bishop Flavin, president of the Institute on Religious Life, has expressed it very beautifully:

> Because religious life is God's gift to the Church, the whole Church, all of God's people, laity as well as clergy and religious, are responsible for the preservation of religious life that it might not lose its power to pay homage to God, to sanctify souls and to serve all the needs of the people of God.[52]

NOTES

[1]Rev. James Hennessey, S.J., *American Catholics* (New York: Oxford University Press, 1981), p. 329.

[2]Kenneth Baker, S.J., "Papal Study of American Seminaries," *Homiletic & Pastoral Review*, January 1982.

[3]Koopman, Joop, *National Catholic Register*, March 21, 1982, p. 1.

[4]Robert, G. Howes, "The Parish Priest: Endangered Species?," *Homiletic & Pastoral Review*, November 1982, p. 20.

[5]Bernadette Counihan, O.S.F. "Is There a Solution to the Vocation Crisis?," *Homiletic & Pastoral Review*, February 1978, p. 51. The number of nuns in the U.S. has dropped from 179,000 in 1965 to 120,000 in 1983. See "Rome, U.S. Nuns Eye its Future," *National Catholic Register*, Oct. 9, 1983, p. 1.

[6]William C. McCready, "Attitudes Toward the Vocations to the Priestly and Religious Life," *Young Catholics* (New York: Sadlier, 1980), p. 127.

[7]McCready, p. 155.

[8]Andrew Greeley, "Sociological Study of the Ministry and Life of the American Priest," *National Conference of Catholic Bishops*, Washington, DC, 1972, p. 313.

[9]Francis J. Spellman, "Three Causes of the Vocation Shortage," *Catholic Star Herald*, February 12, 1982.

[10]Cited in "Three Causes of the Vocation Shortage," *Catholic Digest*, July 1982, p. 32.

[11]Rev. Kenneth Baker, S.J., "Papal Study of American Seminaries," *Homiletic & Pastoral Review*, January 1982, p. 80.

[12]"And Where are the Bishops?," letter to the editor, *HPR*, July 1982, p. 7.

[13]McCready, p. 155.

[14]Dolores Curran, "Whatever Happened to Good Ol' Catholic Families," *God, Religion and Family Life*, David Thomas, ed. (St. Meinrad, IN: Abbey Press, 1979), p. 20.

[15]"Decree on the Ministry and Life of Priests," *Vatican II*, 6.

[16]To the bishops of the Ivory Coast, November 19, 1981.

[17]Pope John Paul II, *Familiaris Consortio* (Ottawa: Canadian Conference of Catholic Bishops), p. 99.

[18]Pope John Paul II, "The Role of the Family in the Birth of Vocations," *L'Osservatore Romano*, January 25, 1982, p. 5.

[19]Quoted by Samuel Coale in "Marriage in Contemporary American Literature: The Mismatched Marriages of Manichean Minds," *Thought*, March 1983, p. 115.

[20]Michael Windolph, "What Vocation Crisis?," *HPR*, June 1982, p. 19.

[21]*New York Times*, January 6, 1982, p. 12.

[22]John J. Mulloy, "Annulling the Institution of Marriage," *The Wanderer*, February 11, 1982, p. 4.

[23]Paul Cole Beach, "Marriage and the Crisis of Divorce," *HPR*, March 1981, p. 53.

[24]*Ibid.*

[25]Judith S. Wallerstein and Joan B. Kelly, "Children and Divorce," *Social Work*, 24, (Nov. 1979) 6: p. 469.

[26]Heather L. Ross and Isabel V. Sawhill, *Time of Transition: The Growth of Families Headed by Women* (n.p.: Urban Institute, 1975), p. 132.

[27]Wallerstein, p. 469.

[28]Godfrey Poage and John Treacy, *Parents' Role in Vocations* (Milwaukee: Bruce, 1959).

[29]Basil Pennington, O.C.S.O., "Vocation Awareness in the Light of the Church's Mission," *Sisters Today*, June-July, 1980, p. 668.

[30]J.B. Orr, "The Changing Family: A Social Ethical Perspective," in *Changing Images of the Family*, V. Tuftee and B. Myerhoff, eds. (New Haven: Yale University Press, 1980), p. 380.

[31]*The Documents of Vatican II*, W. Abbott, S.J., ed. (New York: The America Press, 1966), p. 481.

[32]Mary Theresa Glynn, R.S.M., "Why I Came, Why I Stay," *Sisters Today*, January 1979, p. 303.

[33]*The Documents*, p. 468.

[34]James Hitchcock, "Where Religious Life Still Flourishes," *Columbia*, August 1982, p. 10.

[35]Counihan, p. 53.

[36]Thomas Dubay, S.M., *America*, March 13, 1976.

[37]See Thomas Dubay, S.M., "Religious Life: The Real Polarity," *Review for Religious*, May 1973.

[38]Joseph H. Fichter, S.J., *Religion as an Occupation* (Notre Dame, IN: University of Notre Dame Press, 1961), p. 35.

[39]E. Doyle McCarthy, "Sociology and the Changing Image of the Family," *Thought*, March 1983, p. 96.

[40]Vatican City (AP) as reported in the *Kitchener-Waterloo Record*, Sept. 6, 1983.

[41]Alfred De Manche, "Some Disturbing Trends," *The Catholic Register*, April 30, 1983.

[42]*K-W Record.*

[43]Windolph, p. 21.

[44]*Familiaris Consortio*, sec. 17, p. 33.

[45]Charles A. Gallagher, "The Mission of the Family," *The Way*, Spring 1983, p. 124.

[46]*Lumen Gentium*, 1.

[47]*Ibid.*, 11.

[48]Kenneth Baker, S.J., "The 1980 Synod on the Family," *HPR*, Feb. 1981, p. 15.

[49]*Familiaris Consortio*, 21, p. 40. See also *Apostolicam Actuositatem*, 11.

[50]*Mystici Corporis*, June 29, 1943.

[51]*Perfectae Caritatis*, 7.

[52]Quoted in *Columbia*, August 1982, p. 19.

9

Transcendentalism
and the Incarnation

The Fourth of July weekend of 1986 provided Americans with an additional reason to express their patriotic fervor. Along with the usual celebration of Independence Day was the concelebration of the 100th anniversary of the Statue of Liberty. And to stir the excitement to even greater heights, America's most cherished image of freedom was undraped to reveal the spectacular benefits of a $40 million face-lift, an operation that seemed to justify its popular personification as "The Lady."

At the conclusion of its prime-time coverage of the lavish "liberty weekend," and while the sound of America's noisiest pyrotechnical extravaganza was still ringing in the ears of its viewers, ABC television spotlighted a man who embodies the American spirit of liberty and independence—Henry David Thoreau. The camera followed him as he walked briskly and defiantly along the edge of Walden Pond. He was doing something he could not have done in the middle of the nineteenth century, reciting his own prose to a crew of pursuing technicians. The sequence ended as he delivered the now too familiar lines of his anthem to individualism: "If a man does not keep pace with his companions, perhaps it is because he hears a different drummer. Let him step to the music which he hears, however measured or far away."[1]

Thoreau must have found this phrase much to his liking, for he used it again in his *Journals* (July 1851) in an abbreviated form: "Let a man step to the music which he hears, however measured." It is a good summation in capsule form of his essential philosophy, a stubborn non-conformity combined with a love for independence and a dedication to individualism. Because he embodies these ideals he is presented as the quintessential American.

Yet in another sense, Thoreau is an unlikely person to be singled out as an exemplar for Americans to emulate. His unbending attitude of non-conformity, particularly to his own country and countrymen, is diametrically opposed to patriotism in any meaningful sense. In fact, a reading of his appraisal of humanity leaves one with the unmistakable sense that his misanthropy must have been severely neurotic. He maintained that "Society is always diseased, and the best is the silliest."[2] He defined "good fellowship" as "the virtue of pigs in a litter, which lie close together to keep warm."[3] He could condemn humanity on a regional basis, as when he exclaimed that "There is nothing to redeem the bigotry and moral cowardice of New Englanders in my eyes," or universally as when he wrote: "It appears to me that, to one standing on the heights of philosophy, mankind and the works of man will have sunk out of sight altogether."[4] Moreover, his vitriol against mankind often had a fevered and excessive quality to it that said more about him than about humanity: "Yesterday I was influenced with [sic] the rottenness of human relations. They appeared full of death and decay, and offended the nostrils."[5] "It is pleasant to meet the dry yellowish-colored fruit of the poison dogwood . . ., it has so much character relatively to man."[6]

One must ask the question, "who indeed is the drummer Thoreau heard?" A different drummer—no doubt. But one worthy of setting a pace for an American, a human being? And yet Thoreau is held up and honored as a splendid personification of American ideals.

What, then, are these American ideals? They are the abstract, discarnate values of independence, liberty, and individuality. Alone, however, these values may be combined with unpatriotism, irresponsibility, and misanthropy. Noting the shallowness of Americanism, the distinguished Austrian psychiatrist Viktor Frankl remarked that if the United States has a statue of liberty on the East Coast, it should balance this value with a statue of responsibility on the West Coast.

Thoreau and Americanism converge in Transcendentalism. They both offer the highest praise to one-sided ideals that, though lofty and inspirational in their own right, are bereft of their complementary and counterbalancing opposites, and consequently are thin and dangerous. They are, as Thoreau himself referred to them, the "higher laws." But they are not real laws, that is, laws by which men can live together in peace, harmony, and mutual respect. They are the exhilarating illusions of pseudo-mysticism. Henry James was demonstrating his gift for clear perception when he said of Thoreau:

> Whatever question there may be of his talent, there can be none, I think, of his genius. It was a slim and crooked one....
> He was unperfect, unfinished, inartistic; he was worse than provincial—he was parochial.[7]

How can someone as parochial as Thoreau be considered patriotic? Only, it would seem, if America's ideals are themselves parochial. But by "parochial" we mean in the philosophical sense, of being too limiting, of not embracing all of the relevant values at once. One is philosophically parochial if he adopts freedom without responsibility, independence without community, or nature without human fellowship. James Russell Lowell, the most respected literary critic of Thoreau's time, was appalled by Henry David's shallowness and his anti-social stance that deprived him of the benefits of social intercourse:

> It is a very shallow view that affirms trees and rocks to be healthy, and cannot see that men in communities are just as

> true to the laws of their organization and destiny; that can
> tolerate the puffin and the fox, but not the fool and the
> knave; that would shun politics because of its demagogues,
> and snuff up the stench of the obscene fungus.[8]

> The radical vice of his theory of life was, that he confounded
> physical with spiritual remoteness from men. One is far
> enough withdrawn from his fellows if he keeps himself clear
> of their weaknesses. He is not so truly withdrawn as exiled,
> if he refuse to share in their strength. It is a morbid self-
> consciousness that pronounces the world of men empty and
> worthless before trying it. . . .[9]

Other critics are similarly unsparing in their denunciation of
Thoreau's narrowness. Robert Louis Stevenson said that "He
was not easy, not ample, not urbane, not even kind; his
enjoyment was hardly smiling, or the smile was not broad enough
to be convincing . . . he was all improved and sharpened to a
point."[10] Brooks Atkinson refers to the first chapter of *Walden* as
"pure truculence,"[11] while Alfred Kazin saw it as "self-
dramatizing."[12] Others saw Thoreau as a "sophist and
sentimentalizer" and "an author who exaggerates the importance
of his own thoughts."[13]

Thoreau was a man who "never found a companion so
companionable as solitude."[14] He never voted, refused to pay
taxes to the state, and renounced everything traditional,
conventional, and socially acceptable. He is not a patriotic hero
as much as an embarrassingly painful index of the utter
shallowness and one-sidedness of the American dream.

"Lady Liberty" is 100 years old. In the perspective of history,
however, she is very young. In fact, we might regard her as a
nubile adolescent who is looking forward to meeting her mate.
She is "carrying the torch," so to speak, but for a reason other
than the one commonly understood.

Thoreau, in his chosen one-sidedness, naturally rejected the
incarnational values that Christianity represented. "I had rather
keep bachelor's hall in hell than go to board in heaven," he once

exclaimed. "The church! it is eminently the timid institution, and the heads and pillars of it are constitutionally and by principal the greatest cowards in the community."[15] Walter Harding remarks that Thoreau substituted "beauty, goodness, and truth" for the Christian Trinity,[16] an exchange that sacrificed the personal for the abstract. Thoreau was not a man who wanted to touch people. He complained that "we live thick and are in each other's way, and stumble over one another," and recommended that there be "but one inhabitant to a square mile."[17] "The value of man is not in his skin," he asserted, "that we should touch him."[18] Thoreau, his individuality notwithstanding, had not succeeded in immunizing himself against the Puritanical values that had saturated his New England culture for so long.

Not even his beloved world of nature was particularly substantial for Thoreau. "The universe is unreal," he wrote, "It is only an emanation of God put forth through the mind of man." He was a transcendentalist through and through. For him the solidest realities were the loftiest dreams of his imagination. "My genius makes distinctions," he tells us, "which my understanding cannot and which my senses do not report."[19] He was an idealist who regarded the rabble of the senses something that the mind and the imagination had to transcend. His world was not *terra firma*, but an idealized, Platonic realm that nature intimated.

There is no saint in the hagiography of the Catholic Church who better exemplifies the importance of touch than St. Francis of Assisi. The story is told of how, when Francis first touched a leper, and even kissed the fingers of the sick man, a sweetness, happiness, and joy streamed into his soul. According to one of his biographers, Johannes Jörgensen, by overcoming his repugnance to touching the most repulsive of men, Francis gained the greatest victory man can win—a victory over oneself.[20] The chronicles of the life of St. Francis tell stories of other instances where he touched lepers and miracles of healing took place.[21] Moreover, the stigmata that Francis suffered is God's penetrating touch that has both physical as well as sacramental significance.

As one writer has stated, "St. Francis was the very antithesis of a sour Puritan."[22] In contradistinction with Thoreau, Francis wanted to be with people. He founded communities, rebuilt churches, anointed the sick, and begged food from door to door. Francis was intensely tactile and had nothing of the Puritan in him.

At the same time, there are superficial similarities between Francis and Thoreau that could very easily mislead people into thinking that they were cut from the same cloth. They both shared a love of nature and an affection for animals. Both were poets for whom the sun had a central and richly symbolic meaning. They both warned against the dangers of prosperity and even property. They were eccentric individualists who were strikingly at odds with conventional society. They denounced superfluous wants and identified freedom as needing less and less. Francis embraced poverty wholeheartedly, whereas Thoreau came within $.27 per week of this ideal while he was living in his one-room hut by Walden Pond—"as he simplifies his life, the laws of the universe will appear less complex, solitude will not be solitude, nor poverty poverty, nor weakness weakness."[23] Dwelling on their similarities, one might be led to suspect that Thoreau was a lay Franciscan.

They also have sundry other and more trivial things in common. Both died in their mid-forties after being sick for much of their lives. Neither one married. Each one is known for his ecological concerns (Pope John Paul II named Francis the patron saint of ecology in 1980). And both have been honored in countless diverse ways from being the subjects of children's books, and appearing on United States postage stamps, to inspiring major piano works: Francis for Franz Liszt's "St. François d'Assise: Prédication aux oiseaux" and Thoreau for Charles Ives' "Concord Sonata."

St. Francis anticipated so many attitudes that are congenial to the modern mind, in fact, some of the very attitudes that Henry David Thoreau himself espoused. Yet Francis is not a Modernist, but a Christian, not a transcendentalist, but a disciple of the Incarnation.

Thoreau's religious stance has been described as pantheistic.[24] This does not seem to be an unfair assessment considering what Thoreau has expressed on the subject. His God does not appear to be a personal God or even a transcendent one. For Thoreau, God is identifiable with nature, nature being the only source of sanity, the only cure for human ills:

> In my Pantheon, Pan still reigns in his pristine glory, with his ruddy face, his flowing beard, and his shaggy body, his pipe and his crook . . . for the great god Pan is not dead, as was rumored. Perhaps of all the gods of New England and of ancient Greece, I am most constant at his shrine.[25]

> I have come to this hill to see the sun go down, to recover sanity and put myself again in relation with Nature.[26]

> Nature, the earth itself, is the only panacea.[27]

Thoreau, then, to extend his pun on Pan, is a pantheist in whose Pantheon Pan provides the only panacea. Here is a religious narrowness which is the perfect mirror image of the narrowness of his individualism. Just as he expects too much of the exiled individual, he requires mere nature to do the work of God. But man is not complete without society, and nature would not exist without God.

Chesterton points out in his biography of St. Francis that a worship of Pan could lead only to panic and ultimately to pandemonium:

> I too have lived in Arcady; but even in Arcady I met one walking in a brown habit who loved the woods better than Pan. . . .[28]

> Pan was nothing but panic.[29]

Chesterton saw all too clearly, as did Francis, the mistake of nature-worship, the mistake of being natural. Man is a fallen creature, one who stands in need of redemption. Mere nature, which is also flawed in a fundamental way, is powerless to save or cure him. In depending on mere nature, or pure reason, or naked individuality for redemption we do not find a panacea but invite panic. The world's naive confidence in nature led to panic; it needed the glad news of the Gospel about the reality of original sin. According to Chesterton, Francis appeared on the scene at a fortuitous moment in history when men had lost faith in nature and were open to the meaning of the Incarnation. It was Francis, appropriately, who was the first to honor the Babe of Bethlehem by creating the *presepio*, or manger scene.

Christ came to redeem fallen man. He descended into the race of men by taking on human flesh. He did this to provide the way of man's ascent. Both Christ and the Christian of Assisi thus had a special love for the downtrodden. Francis always showed an excited eagerness to help them. He understood the central implication of the Incarnation that if we are to be followers of Christ, we must descend and live among the lowly. Francis was always uniting himself with his brothers as the Word united itself with human flesh in the person of Christ.

Francis understood this descent as an act of courtesy that all men owed each other. It was a courtesy or politeness that imitated the same quality in God. In Francis' own words:

La Cortesia è una delle proprietà di Dio.

The word *Cortesia* was derived from the French and connoted all the chivalry of knighthood that had flowered in France. Courtesy for Francis was a property of God. God not only loves man, but He has the gracious courtesy to descend into human flesh and dwell among men. Courtesy, then, is not merely etiquette or romance; it is a divine attribute. It describes the quality in God that allows Him to be gracious to sinful man. In response to God's graciousness, man should show gratitude.

The courtesy of Francis flowed from the graciousness of God who expressed His divine Courtesy through the Incarnation. Francis could embrace imperfection with hope because he understood the redemptive meaning the Incarnation conveyed. Thoreau, on the other hand, eschewed the company of men and could not tolerate their imperfections because he could not recognize the flaw that was in himself. He was fastidious and did not believe that the tainted or wretched could be loved. Thus, he did not understand the courtesy of God and sought God in the impersonal world of nature.

Both Francis and Thoreau preached the simple life. But Thoreau tried to make things more simple than they could be. Thus, he separated himself from society, nature from God, and love from courtesy. Francis was by far the more realistic and held these values together because the central inspiration of his life was the Incarnation. We should make things as simple as possible, but not simpler. The simple life need not be an impoverished one, but life that does not burden itself by possessing or desiring things that it does not need. The simplicity of Francis is more realistic than that of Thoreau. Francis affirmed both the flesh and the spirit; Thoreau, however, avoided the flesh and idealized the spirit.

Despite Thoreau's posturing about freedom, it was, thanks to the Incarnation, Francis who was truly free. Francis was free to recognize the presence of sin in himself and others because he had faith in Christ's redemption. And he could love and serve people who exhibited glaring weaknesses and imperfections because he emulated the courtesy of God. Thus, he was free to advance in God's grace and to love his neighbor as himself. In this regard, his freedom is not merely independence or freedom *from* something; it has a positive quality that unites him with the life of God and man. In contrast, Thoreau's drummer led him away from things. "I am a mystic,"[30] he proclaimed. But he was a mystic without being anything else. He sought that vague something he called "the higher law," but without embracing ordinary men and their common life. He tried to become a mystic without first being a man. He repeated the mistake of a sect call the Fraticelli, who declared themselves to be the true sons of St. Francis, yet proceeded to denounce marriage and denounce mankind.

The fundamental difference between Francis and Thoreau is the former's acceptance of the essential message of the Incarnation, that the highest does not stand without the lowest, and that the path to Paradise must pass through Bethlehem. Humility, therefore, is primary. But it is just as important to remember that the lowest *does* pass to the highest. Thoreau sought the highest directly and became ensnared in a stifling pantheism.   Francis saw, radiating through the lowest, the transcendent image of God the Father. Dietrich von Hildebrand provides a brilliant insight into this paradox in his little book, *Not As the World Gives*, which is written as St. Francis' message to today's laymen. He states that the inexpressible joy that filled Francis' heart as he beheld the sun, the moon, and the stars was the very opposite attitude of a pantheist. "St. Francis loved all these things, not as if he felt himself in a living oneness with 'Mother Nature'; but he loved them all because he saw all creatures as coming from the heavenly Father, 'whose wonders the heavens praise.'"[31] Thoreau sought the heavens, but did not know that there was something higher, that even the heavens praised. Francis embraced the immediacy of God's Motherhood in nature without ever losing sight of His transcendent Fatherhood. Francis loved and served with boundless joy, the one God whose own being could neither be contained by the immanent nor exhausted by the eternal. He loved the Incarnate Christ whose very being is perfect praise of the Mother and the Father.

NOTES

[1]Henry David Thoreau, *Walden & Civil Disobedience*, Owen Thomas, ed. (New York: W.W. Norton, 1966), p. 215.

[2]*Journals*, I: p. 306; 1841.

[3]*J.* IV: p. 397.

[4]*J.* III: pp. 381-2; 1852.

[5]*J.* IV: p. 472; 1853.

[6]*J.* II: p. 128; 1850.

[7]Henry James, in *Hawthorne*, 1879, Ch. I.

[8]James Russell Lowell, "Thoreau," Walter Harding, ed., *Thoreau: A Century of Criticism* (Dallas; Southern Methodist University Press, 1965), p. 50.

[9]*Ibid.*, p. 48.

[10]Robert Louis Stevenson, "Henry David Thoreau: His Character & Opinions," in Harding, 1965, p. 59.

[11]Walter Harding, *A Thoreau Handbook* (New York: New York University Press, 1961), p. 24.

[12]Alfred Kazin, "Thoreau's Journals" in Harding, 1965, p. 191.

[13]"Thoreau's *Walden*," in Harding, 1965, p. 4.

[14]*Walden*, V.

[15]*J.* XI: p. 325.

[16]Harding, 1961, p. 155.

[17]*Walden*, V.

[18]*Ibid.*

[19]*J.* II: p. 337.

[20]Johannes Jörgensen, *St. Francis of Assisi* (Garden City, NY: Doubleday, 1959), p. 39.

[21]*The Mirror of Perfection*, chaps. 44 & 58; *The Little Flowers*, chap. 25; "And the miracle divine, whenever St. Francis touched him with his holy hands the leprosy departed, and the flesh became perfectly whole."

[22]Thomas Okey, "Introduction," *The Little Flowers, etc.* (London: Dent & Sons, 1947), p. XVIII.

[23]*Walden*, "Conclusion"; p. 214. See also *J.*, March 11, 1856. It cost Thoreau $28.12 to build his hut by Walden Pond where he lived on $.27 per week.

[24]George Ripley in Harding, 1965, p. 3.

[25]*Ibid.*, p. 5 where it is quoted from *Walden*.

[26]*J.*, VI: p. 329.

[27]*J.*, XII: p. 350.

[28]G.K. Chesterton, *St. Francis of Assisi* (Garden City, NY: Doubleday, 1952), p. 17.

[29]*Ibid.*, p. 31.

[30]Quoted in Harding, 1965, p. 90.

[31]Dietrich von Hildebrand, *Not As the World Gives* (Chicago: Franciscan Herald Press, 1963), p. 34.

10

The Realism
of Mary's Motherhood

Mary is, as Coventry Patmore has reminded us, "Our only Saviour from an abstract Christ." There is implied in this remark a profound and original notion of motherhood that our present society is in danger of losing. Mary conceived Christ, carried Him under her heart, and gave birth to Him. Through her flesh she gave her Son flesh. In her initial and physical act of mothering Christ, she provided God with a human form, one through which He could grow and feel and suffer as other humans do. She allowed the transformation of a God that we could not see or touch into one who was palpably human and identifiably one of us. She saved us from having to worship an exclusively abstract God. But she has saved us from something else which may be no less important. She has saved us from abstract motherhood.

Mary's motherhood, like all motherhood, is inextricably interwoven with matter. It is by no mere coincidence that the words mother (*mater*) and matter (*materia*) are etymologically related. With motherhood, unlike God's creation, there is a carnal link with new life which justifies repeated comparisons with the fertility of nature. Gerard Manley Hopkins has said of the natural affinity she bears for everything which flows from her motherhood:

All things rising, all things sizing
Mary sees, sympathizing
With that world of good,
Nature's motherhood.[1]

St. Alphonsus de Liguori finds in the *Song of Songs*—"Thy belly is like a heap of wheat, set about with lilies"—an important and revealing allusion to Mary's motherhood.[2] To corroborate his view, he cites the authority of St. Ambrose who explains this passage by remarking "That although in the most pure womb of Mary there was but one grain of corn, which was Jesus Christ, yet it is called a heap of wheat because all the elect were virtually contained in it."[3]

The image of wheat also implies the Eucharist, since wheat is the original matter which is eventually transubstantiated into the Body of Christ. Not only does the matter of Mary's womb bear Christ, but the bread on the altar also bears him. The material link between Mary's body and our spiritual food which is the Body of Christ, is beautifully and succinctly expressed by St. Augustine when he states that "she gave milk to our Bread."[4]

The material concreteness of Christianity, which begins in the Word being made flesh in Mary's womb, extends beyond the Sacraments and includes the sacramentals. What the Eucharist is in the order of Sacraments, the Rosary is in the order of sacramentals. As Fulton Sheen has pointed out, "The mark of the Christian is the willingness to look for the Divine in the flesh of a babe in a crib, the continuing Christ under the appearance of bread on an altar, and a meditation and a prayer on a string of beads."[5] But the womb also prefigures Christ's crucifixion:

The Savior left high heaven to dwell
    Within the Virgin's womb;
And there arrayed himself in flesh,
    Our Victim to become.[6]

At the same time, the incarnation also foreshadows the resurrection and ascension of Christ as well as Mary's assumption. And it was precisely because of this recognition of the sanctity of the flesh that the earliest Christians closed their creed with a profession of faith in the resurrection of the flesh.[7]

Mary has saved us from an abstract Christ. Her motherhood has given Christianity a solid and concrete focus that exists on an objective plane where the subjective activities of pride, egoism, and willfulness cannot distort it or reduce it to a form of self-worship. The intense realism of Mary's motherhood has saved us from an abstract Christianity. But the process has not been easy.

In the very infancy of the Church, a group of heretics known as Docetists denied that Christ had a body and that He was born of a woman. The name Docetist (which was given to them by Ignatius of Antioch) is derived from the Greek word *dokein* which means to appear or to seem. The Docetists taught that Christ's body was a phantom; it had only the appearance, but not the reality of a body. Consequently, his suffering, death, and resurrection were also unreal.

In his letters to the Christians at Ephesus and at Smyrnaea, Ignatius referred to the basic problem that confronted the Docetists as the scandal of the flesh (*scandalum carnis*). For the Docetists, it was a blasphemous apotheosis of the flesh to believe that the Word took flesh from a woman, that the Eucharist was enfleshed, and that the flesh was capable of immortal life.

The abhorrence of the flesh, which runs through Docetist teaching is strongly influenced by the thought of Zoroaster, a Persian who lived five centuries prior to the Christian era. Zoroaster held that Spirit and Matter, Light and Darkness, Good and Evil were irreconcilable.

Following the Docetists, the Gnostics took an equally negative view of the body. One of their leading spokesmen, Saturninus, taught that marriage and procreation are of Satan. Marcion, another influential exponent of Gnosticism, insisted that Christ had no mother. In the fourth century, a sect known as Manichaeans preached that Jesus was in no sense the child of

Mary. The Albigensians of the twelfth century taught that Mary is merely a symbol or a channel through which Christ passed, taking nothing of her flesh.

The Church countered past heresies which rejected the full reality of Mary's motherhood strongly and clearly. At the Council of Alexandria, for example, it is stated: "If anyone does not confess that Emmanuel is true God, and that therefore the holy Virgin is Mother of God (*Dei genetricem—Theotokos*), since she bore, after the flesh, the incarnate Word of God, let him be anathema."[8]

The Church has always taken great pride in the motherhood of Mary. In her great hymn of praise—*Te Deum laudamus*—we find these words addressed to Christ: "*Tu ad liberandum suscepturus hominem, non horruisti Virginis uterum*" (Thou, when about to undertake man's deliverance, didst not draw back in horror of the Virgin's womb). Even those outside the pale of Catholicism often paid deep homage to the Virgin's motherhood. Nathaniel Hawthorne once wrote: "I have always envied the Catholics that sweet, sacred, Virgin Mother who stands between them and the Deity, intercepting somewhat His awful splendor, but permitting His love to stream on the worshipper more intelligibly to human comprehension through the medium of a woman's tenderness."

In the present era, however, we still find, even among Christian clergymen, a pronounced disdain for the womb. Joseph Fletcher offers a particularly lucid example of this attitude when he states:

> The womb is a dark and dangerous place, a hazardous environment. We should want our potential children to be where they can be watched and protected as much as possible.[9]

Fletcher's denigration of the body (he wants a ban on all childbirth) is the obverse of his unlimited faith in rational control. His view of the body as an obstacle that must be surmounted by technology is reminiscent of Jean-Paul Sartre's appraisal of the body as a "facticity" that impedes human freedom. Sartre's long-time collaborator and close associate, Simone de Beauvoir, has called for the repeal of marriage, an arrangement she contemptuously describes as "an obscene bourgeois institution." De Beauvoir successfully restricted her own motherhood to the domain of the abstract and became the intellectual matriarch of contemporary radical feminism. Her portrayal of the pregnant woman reads like a physician's pathology report:

> Ensnared by nature, the pregnant woman is plant and animal, a stockpile of colloids, an incubator, an egg; she scares children proud of their young, straight bodies and makes young people titter contemptuously because she is a human being, a conscious and free individual, who has become life's passive instrument.[10]

An age which views pregnancy in such stark and sinister terms must find it difficult to appreciate the profound significance of the words "Blessed is the fruit of thy womb" which Elizabeth uttered in greeting her pregnant cousin. These same words, incorporated within the Rosary which Mary taught St. Dominic, and recited over and over again, provided the effective means of converting the Albigensians to an acceptance of Mary's divine maternity. Henry Adams has made the comment, concerning this troublesome era, that "In the bankruptcy of reason, she alone was real."[11]

But the reality of Mary's motherhood and even the reality of motherhood itself is facing a formidable challenge in the present world. Recent advances in reproductive technology have created the impression that there is no real, stable, and objective basis for motherhood. When artificial insemination was introduced in the United States toward the end of the nineteenth century, some of its advocates hailed it as a superior form of sexual congress than conjugal intercourse. One of its more voluble enthusiasts dubbed it "ethereal copulation."[12]   But the real victim of artificial insemination was not sexual intercourse as much as fatherhood. To the man who sells sperm that is later used to fertilize some woman he never meets, his own fatherhood is merely hypothetical, an abstraction. More recent techniques have made it possible to make motherhood seem equally abstract.

A woman can now donate an egg which is fertilized *in vitro*, retain her anonymity, and never know whether her fertilized egg which was subsequently transferred to a second woman resulted in the birth of a child. To the ovum donor, her own motherhood under such circumstances, remains an abstraction. One case in particular allows us to understand not only how reproductive technology can make motherhood appear abstract, but how certain forces in contemporary society want it to be that way and are even proposing legislation that would remove motherhood from the objective plane of reality and relocate it in the subjective domain of the will. Such an attitude must be highly injurious to a real, living Christianity because it attacks the Christian faith at its roots, at its fundamental and realistic basis in the Incarnation of Christ through the Motherhood of Mary.

In a 1986 case, referred to as *Smith v. Jones*, a New York couple's embryo was implanted, after *in vitro* fertilization, into a surrogate mother. The procedure, carried out by Dr. Wulf Utian at Mount Sinai Hospital in Cleveland, was a medical milestone. It marked the first time a surrogate mother gave birth to a child who was originally conceived with the egg and sperm of a couple otherwise unable to have a child.[13]

Because this bifurcation of biological maternity into genetic and gestational phases is novel, existing laws provided no guidance in determining which of these two mothers should be regarded as the legal mother. Since the traditional presumption is that the birthing mother is also the genetic mother, it is her name that routinely appears on the birth certificate. If the genetic mother (who did not gestate the child) is to be recognized as the legal biological mother, she must first adopt the child.

In an apparently unprecedented ruling, however, the Michigan Circuit Court judge declared that the legal biological mother was not the woman who bore the child, but the one who provided the egg that was fertilized *in vitro*.[14] The law in Michigan and in most other states specified that even if she does not contribute genetically to the child, the woman who gives birth is still the mother.

The ovum donor (the genetic mother), pseudonymous Mary Smith, sought to establish her maternity, curiously enough, under Michigan's Paternity Act. Traditionally, this statute had served two purposes. It provided a mechanism by which a putative father who wanted to acknowledge his non-marital child could seek an order of filiation. It also served as a vehicle to establish paternity for the purpose of enforcing child support obligations against a man disavowing fatherhood. The Paternity Act, however, grounded as it is in the biological fact that there can be only one biological father for a particular child, does not provide criteria by which an equitable judgment could be reached in determining which of two biological mothers (genetic and gestational) should be adjudged the legal biological mother.[15] Judge Marianne Battani determined that egg and sperm donors occupy equal positions. Thus, once blood tests verified the genetic mother, the gestational, "traditional," or "birthing mother" was relegated to the position of a "human incubator."[16] Mary Smith alone was declared the biological mother.

There are two revolutionary features about motherhood this case underscores. The first is that "the person from whose womb the child came" can be judged not to be the legal biological mother. The second is a notion of the "surrogate mother" which ascribes to a woman the depersonalized role of an "incubator." There is more than a hint of arbitrariness and willfulness about denying the gestational mother her maternity or resorting to mechanical metaphors in describing her function of carrying a child. Nonetheless, this is an inevitable consequence of using technological modes of reproduction to transfer the basis of

motherhood from the physically intimate realm of conjugal lovers
to the mental world and abstract intentions of infertile couples.

The legal definition of "mother" had traditionally carried an
unshakeable presumption, namely, that she is "the person from
whose womb the child came."[17] Though not articulated as such in
the legal field, this presumption has been so absolute that, until
recently, it has generated no controversy. Traditionally, this
"presumption of biology," which has formed the definition of
motherhood, had been the unquestioned and pervasive rule for
determining the placement of maternal rights and obligations.
But Judge Battani, faced with this unique case, confessed that
the absence of a clearly articulated legal definition of
motherhood left her without guidance. "We really have no
definition of 'mother' in our lawbooks," she declared. "'Mother'
was believed to have been so basic that no definition was deemed
necessary."[18]

In direct response to the *Smith v. Jones* case, several legal
commentators have proposed new definitions of motherhood in
order to accommodate the woman who wants to be known as the
mother.

Lori Andrews, a research attorney for the American Bar
Foundation and author of *New Conceptions: A Consumer's Guide
to the Newest Fertility Treatments*, has advanced the notion of
"preconception" intent.[19] She has expressed the hope that future
court decisions will have taken into consideration the importance
of the infertile couple's "preconception" of the child, that is, its
intention of having a child before contracting with a woman who
would undertake its "biological conception." Michigan Rep.
Richard Fitzpatrick has proposed a bill to be introduced to the
Michigan legislature entitled the "alternative reproduction act"
which calls for "a societal father and a societal mother" who have
all parental rights and responsibilities for a child conceived
through a reproductive technology such as IVF, Embryo
Transfer, or Surrogate Motherhood using Artificial Insemination.
Such "societal parents" are defined as those who engage in a

fertility technique to have a child and *intend* to have parental rights for it regardless of whether the child is biologically related to either one of them.[20]

Writing for the *Yale Law Journal*, Andrea Stumpf seeks to redefine motherhood by allowing "mental conception" to have primacy over "biological conception." Accordingly, she asserts that: "The psychological dimension of procreation precedes and transcends the biology of procreation."[21] "Prior to physical conception of a child, the beginnings of a normal parent-child relationship can come from mental conception, the desire to create a child."[22] For Stumpf, the mental conception of the child on the part of the infertile couple who intend the child has a force and an existential power that can legitimate an infertile woman's claim to motherhood. "The fact that the initiating parents mentally conceived of the child and afforded it existence prior to the surrogate mother's involvement must be acknowledged," she writes.[23] The surrogate mother herself, according to Stumpf, is merely a "third party."

Making will the basis for motherhood is the perfect antithesis of the basis for Mary's motherhood. Will, that is, creaturely will, removes motherhood from a ground in reality and shifts it to an area closely allied to egoism. Conception in the mind, unlike conception in the womb, does not give real existence to the thing it conceives. The androcentric view of a "womb at the top," so to speak, ushered in by the new reproductive technologies, may very well represent male envy or that of rational, technological society, over what they cannot do that a mother does naturally and without effort.

The great danger of making motherhood and, consequently, Christianity, abstract is that it leads directly toward the worshipping of self rather than the worshipping of God. If the basis of religion is in the mind, then it is the mind that is ultimately worshipped. Moreover, it is only through a realistically based religion that its adherents will see fit to refrain from selecting and rejecting doctrines according to their own subjective preferences. The realism of Mary's motherhood draws us toward her Son, toward reality, toward truth and love. Her maternity—far from being a phantom—makes our own acts whose goodness is derived through her, seem ghost-like by comparison. In the words of the poet Hopkins:

> If I have understood
> She holds high motherhood
> Towards all our ghostly good.[24]

Mary's motherhood does not negate our will, but it invites us to conform our will, as she did, to the will of God. Therein is our freedom, self-realization, and peace. In Dante's celebrated line from his *Paradiso*: "In His will is our peace."[25] Our intensely individualistic culture finds it extremely difficult to understand that a person whose actions are based on arbitrary self-will or instincts or desire is not truly free. Individualism is the expression of an immature will and consequently lacks freedom.

Individualism, as Berdyaev has pointed out, is the "tragedy of empty freedom."[26] Individualism is the desire rising from the ego for something that does not exist. But the Christian desires what does exist, what is real. The former chooses *nothingness*, the latter chooses *being*. Individualism wants what it wants, motherhood, for example, even when there is no objective basis for it. The real mother loves her child. Henry Adams remarked that Mary "cared for her baby, a simple matter, which any woman could do and understand. That, and the grace of God, had made her Queen of Heaven."[27] By contrast, a feminist poet offers an apt description of empty freedom that leads to nothingness when she writes: "I fear the barnacle which might latch on and not let go—so I keep my womb empty and full of possibilities."[28]

Eve desired something that was not possible. Thus, she was not acting realistically when she acted on that desire. Her individualism was the opposite of the universalism of Mary; it severed her relationship with God, whereas Mary's *fiat* not only united her with God but brought Him to all mankind. Eve's individualism was a disunion from the universe, a choice for self-idolization. Mary chose God and that choice affirmed herself in the fullness of her being. According to Aquinas: "Eve sought the fruit, but did not find there what she wished for. In her fruit the blessed Virgin found all that Eve had wanted."[29]

"Zero, by itself, has no value," remarked St. Thérèse of Lisieux, "but put alongside *one* it becomes potent, always provided it is put on the *proper* side, after, and not before. . . ." This simple, yet astute comment offers an ingenious explanation of the emptiness of individualism and the fullness of a life in union with God. The individual alone is really a cipher. "Without Me you can do nothing," Christ tells us. By putting God first, all the ciphers that follow serve to magnify the Lord. But all the ciphers in the world, in trying to make God conform to them by putting themselves first, simply accentuate their own irrelevance, their nothingness. Eve put herself first and therefore did not find in the fruit she ate something that could fill her heart. Mary, on the contrary, put God first and bore Christ as the fruit of her womb.

Mary's motherhood introduces to the world a Christian religion whose incarnate realism stands firmly outside of pride and egoism, those enemies of the human soul which cry out for a redeemer. Mary offers us the realism of the flesh and the realism of an enfleshed Savior. Moreover, her will, in being united with the Divine Will, refutes the emptiness of mere individualism and affirms the fullness of a relationship with God. She saves us from an abstract Christianity, and an abstract conception of motherhood. She saves us from the torment of worshipping ourselves. She touches us with her tenderness and envelopes us in her maternity. She is always the doctor of realism. And the organic wholeness that she expresses through her motherhood is a healing remedy for our relentlessly rational and technological society that, in trying to make a God of reason, succeeds only in making God appear unreasonable. She commends her Son to us with all the irresistible persuasiveness of a loving mother whose favor we should find exceedingly difficult to refuse.

NOTES

[1]G.M. Hopkins, "The May Magnificat," *Gerard Manley Hopkins: Poems and Prose*, W.H. Gardner, ed. (New York: Penguin Books, 1953), p. 38.

[2]*"Venter tuus sicut acervus tritici, vallatus liliis," Cant.* vii, 2.

[3]Alphonsus de Liguori, *The Glories of Mary* (Brooklyn: Redemptorist Fathers, 1931), p. 48.

[4]*Sermons*, 184.

[5]Fulton J. Sheen, *The World's First Love* (Garden City, NY: Doubleday, 1956), p. 181.

[6]*Coelo Redemptor praetulit* (Feast of the Motherhood, eighteenth century).

[7]See Paul F. Palmer, S.J., "Mary and the Flesh," T. Burke, S.J., ed., *Mary and Modern Man* (New York: America Press, 1954), pp. 110-140.

[8]Council of Alexandria, Anathema I of St. Cyril (430).

[9]Joseph Fletcher, *The Ethics of Genetic Control* (Garden City, NY: Doubleday, 1974), p. 103. There is a curious resonance between Fletcher's phrase—"The womb is a dark and dangerous place"—and a line appearing in Andrew Marvell's poem, *To His Coy Mistress*: "The grave's a fine and private place." One has to wonder whether Fletcher, like the Docetists who long preceded him, believed that the womb is more to be feared than the tomb.

[10]Simone de Beauvoir, *The Second Sex* (New York: Grosset & Dunlap, 1968), p. 467.

[11]Henry Adams, *Mont-Saint-Michel & Chartres* (New York: Doubleday, 1959), p. 361.

[12]Robert Francoeur, *Utopian Motherhood: New Trends in Human Reproduction* (London: George Allen & Unwin, 1971), p. 5.

[13]Nancy Blodgett, "Who is Mother? Genetic Donor, Not Surrogate," *American Bar Association Journal*, June 1, 1986, p. 18.

[14]*Smith v. Jones*, No. 85-53201402 (Mich. Cir. Ct., Wayne County), March 14, 1986.

[15]Shari O'Brien, "The Itinerant Embryo and the Neo-Nativity Scene: Bifurcating Biological Motherhood," 1987 *Utah Law Review* (1987), p. 15.

[16]No. 85-532014 DZ, slip. op. at 9.

[17]Andrea E. Stumpf, "Redefining Mother: A Legal Matrix for New Reproductive Technologies," 96 *Yale Law Journal* (Nov. 1986), p. 188.

[18]"Surrogate Has Baby Conceived in Laboratory," *The New York Times*, April 17, 1986, p. A26, col. 4. See also Goodman, "High Technology Redefines Motherhood," *Toledo Blade*, April 25, 1986, p. 9, col. 3.

[19]Blodgett.

[20]*Ibid.*

[21]Stumpf, p. 194.

[22]*Ibid.*, p. 195.

[23]*Ibid.*, p. 205. "Mental conception," needless to say, does not have within itself the power of conferring existence upon the thing it conceives. Only in God are conception and creation (or idea and act) perfectly unified. Stumpf disembodies and de-sexes man and then asks law to treat him as if he were a God.

[24]Hopkins, "The Blessed Virgin Compared To The Air We Breathe," p. 56.

[25]Dante, *Paradiso* III, 85: "*E'n la sua voluntade e nostra pace.*"

[26]Nicolas Berdyaev, *The Meaning of the Creative Act* (New York: Harper & Row, 1962), p. 142.

[27]Adams, p. 366.

[28]Erica Jong.

[29]Thomas Aquinas, *Exposition of the Hail Mary*.

Why another book about C.S. Lewis?

The answer is simple.

C.S. Lewis: A Critical Essay is the most concise and vivid introduction to the life and writings of the greatest Christian apologist of this century. First published twenty years ago, and now revised and updated, Dr. Kreeft's book wisely allows Lewis to speak for himself through a series of judiciously chosen quotations. *C.S. Lewis: A Critical Essay* is a memorable tribute from a contemporary apologist — whose own writings have often been compared to those of Lewis — to his acknowledged Master. (1988, paper, $5.95)

Christendom College Press presents . . .

The Catholic Milieu
by Thomas Storck

In our secular and "pluralistic" society, can there—or should there—exist a culture which is specifically Catholic? Should the Catholic faith be a private matter, a purely interior set of convictions? Thomas Storck, in this brief but provocative study, holds that Catholic truth must be incarnated in our mores, manners, and customs if we are to experience the fullness of Catholic faith. "The establishment of a Catholic culture," Storck concludes, "is the external aspect of St. Pius X's call 'to restore all things in Christ,' the necessary outward complement of Christ's reign in individual hearts." Drawing on the thought of Hilaire Belloc and Christopher Dawson, Storck examines the role of economics and technology on our way of life, and how these systems may be guided toward the common good. Far from proposing a single form of Catholic culture, Storck holds that the universality of the Faith produces a wonderful variety of traditions and practices. If body and soul, public and private, are once more to be reconciled, Storck reminds us, we must learn to inhabit a truly Catholic milieu. **(80 pp., paper, $5.95)**

Please send me ——copy(ies) of **The Catholic Milieu** by Thomas Storck. I enclose my check or money order in **U.S. FUNDS ONLY** for $5.95 plus $1.50 shipping and handling for each copy. (Virginia residents please add 4 1/2% sales tax.) **Please allow four to six weeks for delivery.**

NAME————————————————————————————

ADDRESS———————————————————————————

—————————————————————————————————

CHRISTENDOM COLLEGE PRESS   *FRONT ROYAL, VA 22630*

Christendom College Press
presents
Faith & Reason

Faith & Reason is a quarterly academic journal edited by Timothy T. O'Donnell, S.T.D. Each issue includes many interesting and timely articles by prominent Catholic Scholars such as:

Stanley L. Jaki
Frederick Wilhelmsen
Warren H. Carroll
Jordan Aumann, O.P.
Donald DeMarco
Rev. William G. Most
and others

Each issue also contains reviews of significant books of Catholic interest.

Faith & Reason assists in developing an informed Faith.

If you subscribe now to Faith & Reason, you will receive a year of the best in orthodox Catholic reading plus, as a special bonus, we'll send you our special double issue commemorating the 50th anniversary of the death of G.K. Chesterton. Simply complete the form below and return it with your check.

____ Please enter my subscription to Faith & Reason for 1988.

I enclose: ____ $18.00 regular   ____ $25.00 support subscription

Name_____
Address_____

FAITH & REASON   **ROUTE 3, BOX 87**   **FRONT ROYAL, VA 22630**